W9-BMO-960

THE MORAL DIMENSIONS OF ACADEMIC ADMINISTRATION

ISSUES IN ACADEMIC ETHICS
General Editor: Steven M. Cahn

THE MORAL DIMENSIONS OF ACADEMIC ADMINISTRATION

Rudolph H. Weingartner

ROWMAN & LITTLEFIELD PUBLISHERS, INC.
Lanham • Boulder • New York • Oxford

ROWMAN & LITTLEFIELD PUBLISHERS, INC.

Published in the United States of America
by Rowman & Littlefield Publishers, Inc.
4720 Boston Way, Lanham, Maryland 20706

12 Hid's Copse Road
Cumnor Hill, Oxford OX2 9JJ, England

Copyright © 1999 by Rowman & Littlefield Publishers, Inc.

All rights reserved. No part of this publication may be reproduced,
stored in a retrieval system, or transmitted in any form or by any
means, electronic, mechanical, photocopying, recording, or otherwise,
without the prior permission of the publisher.

British Library Cataloguing in Publication Information Available

Library of Congress Cataloging-in-Publication Data

Weingartner, Rudolph H. (Rudolph Herbert)
    The moral dimensions of academic administration / Rudolph H.
Weingartner.
        p.   cm.—(Issues in academic ethics)
    Includes bibliographical references and index.
    ISBN 0-8476-9096-2 (cloth : alk. paper).—ISBN 0-8476-9097-0
(pbk. : alk. paper)
    1. Education, Higher—Moral and ethical aspects—United States.
    2. —Universities and colleges—United States—Administration.
    3. College teaching—Moral and ethical aspects—United States.
    4. Research—Moral and ethical aspects—United States.   5. College
administrators—Professional ethics—United States.   I. Title.
    II. Series.
    LB2341.W428   1999
    378.1'01—dc21   98-39054
                                                         CIP

Printed in the United States of America

♾ ™ The paper used in this publication meets the minimum requirements of
American National Standard for Information Sciences—Permanence of Paper
for Printed Library Materials, ANSI Z39.48–1984.

Issues in Academic Ethics

Academic life generates a variety of moral issues. These may be faced by students, staff, administrators, or trustees, but most often revolve around the rights and responsibilities of the faculty. In my 1986 book—revised in 1994—*Saints and Scamps: Ethics in Academia* (Rowman & Littlefield), I set out to enumerate, explain, and emphasize the most fundamental of these professional obligations. To do justice to the complexities of academic ethics, however, requires the work of many scholars focused on numerous areas of investigation. The results of such an effort are embodied in this series.

Each volume concentrates on one set of connected issues and combines a single-authored monograph with reprinted sources chosen by the author to exemplify or amplify materials in the text. This format is intended to guide readers while encouraging them to develop and defend their own beliefs.

In recent years philosophers have examined the appropriate standards of conduct for physicians, nurses, lawyers, journalists, business managers, and government policy makers but have not given equal attention to formulating guidelines for their own profession. The time has come to observe the Delphic motto "Know thyself." Granted, the issues in need of critical examination are not exotic, but as the history of philosophy demonstrates, self-knowledge is often the most important to seek and the most difficult to attain.

Steven M. Cahn

This book is for Gissa

Contents

Preface

When Steven Cahn asked me to write a book on academic administration in his series on Issues in Academic Ethics, it was not simply a request to set down my views on that particular topic. In effect, his assignment required that I determine what that topic consisted of in the first place. If you flip to the end of the book, you will see a list of publications referred to in my text, but you won't find any references at all to anything that is actually written on the topic of this book. Accordingly, I felt like a pioneer while writing *The Moral Dimensions of Academic Administration*, with all the hardships and exhilaration pertaining thereto. Working thus on a frontier has also engendered in me two complementary hopes: that readers will find what I have written to be of interest and that others will take up the theme of ethical issues in academic administration and cultivate it further.

Before you plunge into the text, I want to indicate three limits of this book. First, my subject is confined to academic administration in modern American institutions of higher education. While it really does matter that our colleges and universities stand in a tradition that goes back to the Middle Ages, my concern is with the way they have evolved here, in this century. Indeed, I will argue that important obligations of academic administrators derive from the kind of institutions they serve.

Second, since academic administrators are important decision makers in institutions of unusual complexity, one could take the view that the subject of this book should encompass the moral aspects of almost everything that is done in a college or university. This would mean that one might here raise most of the topics that are taken up in each of the books in this series on Issues in Academic Ethics (of which I have seen seven), plus topics in volumes that will or might yet appear. I have not at all been that inclusive, but then I also have not wholly avoided those other issues in academic ethics. Because in the end I was unable to discover a single defensible criterion of inclusion and exclusion, the mundane fact is that I have selected themes I thought to be important to the subject of the moral dimensions of academic administration. What is left out are either themes I thought were well covered elsewhere or topics I did not think to be so very important, or issues I simply failed to think of while I was writing this book. The definite article in the title— *The* Moral Dimensions—thus serves euphony rather than accuracy.

Third, there is no ethical theorizing in what follows this preface, nor are there metaethical discussions. Rather, I talk about obligations and duties of academic administrators, about things they ought to do or refrain from doing—accompanied by sufficient argumentation, I hope, to persuade some readers that I am right in what I claim should be done. Throughout the book, I always *aim* at discussing what are moral obligations. But because academic administration is a *practical* business where *prudentially* there are often better and worse ways of doing things, I no doubt drift into this realm of practical wisdom now and then. And when that is so, a friendly reader will interpret my words as describing practices that are examples—of many other possible ones—of what *ought* (morally) to be done. Kant, in short, is the *eminence grise*. Accordingly, if administrators, reading in this book about their presumed obligations are tempted to demur and say that what is required of them is too difficult, they will know what reply to expect. After all, that it is often more difficult to keep a promise than to break it, to respond to cries for help than to ignore them doesn't change what is the right thing to do.

Finally, a procedural point. Because most readers do not want to pursue references most of the time, I give those in short form as endnotes, with full citations to be found under "References." Because it is a nuisance to come upon interpolated text after having finished reading a chapter—when one must either guess what it pertains to or go back to the text—I place such parenthetical passages as footnotes, at the bottom of the page.

I want to express my debt to two institutions. I am appreciative of the fact that the American Council of Learned Societies appointed me to a committee that made awards (from a grant by the MacArthur Foundation) to meagerly endowed colleges for projects in curricular development. Reading those many applications gave me a much greater awareness of the large sector of not very affluent institutions of higher education in this country and of their missions and problems. But above all, I want here to reiterate (in what is surely the last book I will write on a higher education topic) how grateful I am to Northwestern University—not just for letting me serve as its dean of the College of Arts and Sciences, but for giving me considerable freedom to do and try things. Much of what I know about academic administration was learned at

Northwestern and it was there that I was able to refine considerably my sense of what is central to an academic institution and what is peripheral.

I have debts, as well, to persons. I am very grateful to Kurt Baier, University Professor Emeritus of Philosophy, University of Pittsburgh, and Professor Rosa Pinkus of the University of Pittsburgh Medical School for reading early versions of the early chapters; to James J. Sheehan, the Dickason Professor of Humanities, Stanford University, for reading somewhat later versions of those and some more chapters; and to Kenneth R. Seeskin, Professor of Philosophy, Northwestern University, who read a still later version of the manuscript when it was nearly finished. All of these kind readers assisted me greatly by encouraging me and by making numerous comments and suggestions that helped me to improve the book. That it is not as good as it might be is certainly not their fault!

I am grateful to Steven M. Cahn, not only for the suggestions he made for improving this book, but also, in spite of my agonizing, for asking me to write it in the first place. Somehow— irrationally?—I believe that thinking hard is good for you. That's what I had to do, though I know that such efforts alone do not guarantee respectable results.

Ben Eggleston, a doctoral candidate in philosophy at the University of Pittsburgh, has been immensely helpful throughout the period during which the book was written, digging things up in the library and securing odd items via interlibrary loan. I am very grateful to have had his reliable assistance.

The book is dedicated to my wife, Gissa, who has given me the kind of multidimensional support for which there is no substitute.

Chapter 1

Institutions of Higher Education Have Obligations

I. The Business Corporation and the Institution of Higher Education

Institutions of higher education have obligations because of the kind of institutions they are.* To establish that claim, we first look at IHEs *as* institutions, and begin by contrasting them with business corporations. One prevalent view of the latter holds that this institution has, as such, no moral obligations other than those, like paying debts owed or refraining from cheating customers, that pertain to everyone. Milton Friedman, in a paradigmatic formulation of this position, puts his thesis right into the title: "The Social Responsibility of Business Is to Increase Its Profits."[1] A corporate executive "has direct responsibility to his employers. That responsibility is to conduct the business in accordance with their desires, which generally will be to make as much money as possible, while conforming to the basic rules of society, both those embodied in the law and those embodied in ethical custom."[2] His argument for this thesis is a kind of reductio ad absurdum. To the extent to which executives act in behalf of social causes (presumably because they hold the view that the corporation has obligations to the society of which they are a part), it converts them from agents of the stockholders into public employees, analogous to civil servants. But all this without being subject to political processes—election, control—of any kind. In sum, "the doctrine of 'social responsibility' taken seriously would extend the scope of the political mechanism to every human activity."[3]

Assuming Friedman's view to be adopted—as it is by many[4]—it will nevertheless not shed much light on the responsibilities of IHEs, even

---

*Because of the frequent need to refer to "institutions of higher education," I will adopt the abbreviation IHE for the singular and IHEs for the plural.

though virtually all of them are public corporations. For his account is specific to corporations that are *businesses* while whatever colleges and universities are for, no one is likely to assert that their obligations are to make as much money as possible. But of course by no means does everyone agree with this classical view of business corporations. While there is a large body of literature that puts forward arguments to the effect that they have a variety of social responsibilities,[5] it is sufficient here to refer to but one influential line of argument. It is naive, goes the reasoning, to build a theory of the modern corporation solely on the relationship of its management to its stockholders (even if it would take more nerve than most humans can muster to call Milton Friedman "naive"). A more accurate assessment of what a corporation is requires looking at *all* the categories of people to whom it stands in some significant relationship. Thus, in an article setting forth such a view, a diagram shows a box called "The Corporation" surrounded by and connected to ellipses that circumscribe the words "Management," "Employees," "Owners," "Suppliers," "Customers," and "Local Community."[6] These categories are identified as *stakeholders*, because they are "groups and individuals who benefit from or are harmed by, and whose rights are violated or respected by, corporate actions."[7] The theory is called the stakeholder theory of the corporation.

In our context, this theory constitutes a promising framework for discussion, while at the same time we would be well advised not to be drawn into a *general* discussion of it, as is to be found in the literature on business ethics. For while there are a variety of arguments that support claims to a special relationship between the managers and the owners of a corporation (making Friedman's view the one to beat), I know of no successful arguments of a perfectly *general* kind that support the assertion that a corporation has responsibilities to *unspecified* others or to society *simpliciter*. Instead, arguments must be made piecemeal, in behalf of different specific groups or individuals, to the effect that a corporation has responsibilities toward this or that particular one. Since no general discussion would spare us this task, the stakeholder theory can be regarded as a useful perspective, as specific regions are explored from which an institution might derive certain responsibilities.

Some of the obligations that might be ascribed to colleges and universities will resemble or are identical to those that might be imputed to business corporations. Thus, arguments claiming or denying that IHEs have certain responsibilities toward the communities that house them are likely to resemble those that take up the responsibilities of business corporations toward their immediate environment.[8] However, as we turn to look at the obligations of colleges and universities, we will be less concerned with those they might have in common with businesses than with those that are specific to IHEs and distinguish them from familiar commercial enterprises. But as we turn to explore the sources of moral obligations of academic institutions, we will at least not have the burden of looking over our shoulder at Milton Friedman. As he himself recognizes, "A group of persons might establish a corporation for an eleemosynary purpose—for example, a hospital or a school. The manager of such a corporation will not have money profit as his objective but rendering of certain services."[9] IHEs are exactly of that kind, so that we need not worry whether discharging a responsibility toward some particular group unjustifiably takes away from the stockholders' profits. But we do need to identify the sources of institutional responsibilities and show how those obligations are incurred.

II. Institutions of Higher Education: Their Roots in Society

Individuals put their money into some means of production or commerce and, as we say, go into business. And when that business is incorporated—as is most likely, for that stratagem gives it a life independent of that of the owners and also shields those owners from certain liabilities—the articles of incorporation do not limit what goals the company may pursue. Incorporation creates legal persons to whom quite a few of the capacities of natural persons are given, including the right to engage in any business that is legal. Never mind that the owners first had in mind to make steel, but later decided to make sausages—instead or in addition!

The same is not true of a college or university whether it is private or public. The creation of such an institution not only confers the usual corporate rights on the IHE—such as the right to own property, to enter into contracts, to sue and be sued—but makes a statement of its purposes central to its creation, whether the incorporation is accomplished by charter, by an article in a state's constitution, or by legislation. A selection of excerpts from such originating documents (in America) will give some indication of the different ways in which these purposes are formulated. Look, in particular, at the phrases that have been underlined by this writer.

> George the Third . . . WILL, ordain, grant & constitute that there be a College erected in our said Province of New Hampshire by the name of DARTMOUTH COLLEGE . . . for the education & instruction of Youth of the Indian Tribes in this Land in reading, writing & <u>all parts of Learning</u> which shall appear necessary and expedient for civilizing & christianizing

Children of Pagans as well as in all <u>liberal Arts and Sciences</u>; and also of english Youth and any others.[10]

The objects of the University of Colorado, established by law . . . , shall be to provide the best and most efficient means of imparting to young men and women, on equal terms, a <u>liberal education</u> and thorough knowledge of the <u>different branches of literature, the arts and sciences</u>, with their varied applications. The university, so far as practicable, shall begin the course of study in its collegiate and scientific departments at the points where the same are completed in high schools, and no student shall be admitted who has not previously completed the elementary studies in such branches as are taught in the common schools throughout the state.[11]

Grant Founding and Endowing the Leland Stanford Junior University (Nov. 11, 1885). <u>Its nature, that of a university</u> with such seminaries of learning as shall make it <u>of the highest grade</u>, including mechanical institutes, museums, galleries of art, laboratories, and conservatories, together with all things necessary for the study of agriculture in all its branches, and for the mechanical training, and the <u>studies and exercises directed to the cultivation and enlargement of the mind</u>; Its object, to qualify its students for personal success, and direct usefulness in life; And its purposes, <u>to promote the public welfare by exercising an influence in behalf of humanity and civilization</u>, teaching the blessings of liberty regulated by law, and inculcating love and reverence for the great principles of government as derived from the inalienable rights of man to life, liberty, and the pursuit of happiness.[12]

The University of Wyoming. The objects of such university shall be to provide an efficient means of imparting to young men and young women, without regard to color, on equal terms, <u>a liberal education</u>, together with a thorough <u>knowledge of the various branches connected with the scientific, industrial and professional pursuits</u>. To this end it shall embrace <u>colleges or departments of letters, of science, and of the arts together with such professional or other departments as in the course of time may be connected therewith</u>. The department of letters shall embrace a liberal course of instruction in language, literature and philosophy, together with such courses or parts of courses in the college or department of science as are deemed necessary.[13]

Charter of the Tulane University of Louisiana. Includes the May 2, 1882, letter of Paul Tulane, stating his intention to make the donation that founds the university. [This donation is to be] . . . for the promotion and encouragement of <u>intellectual, moral and industrial education</u> among the white young persons in the city of New Orleans, State of Louisiana, and <u>for the advancement of learning and letters, the arts and sciences therein</u>.

By the term education, I mean to foster such a course of <u>intellectual development as shall be useful and of solid worth</u>, and not merely be ornamental or superficial. I mean you should adopt the course which, as wise and good men, would commend itself to you as being conducive to immediate practical benefit, rather than theoretical possible advantage. I wish you to establish or foster institutions of a higher grade of learning where the young persons to be benefitted shall, upon due examination, be found competent and qualified for admission, both by age and previous training, to receive the benefits of a more advanced degree of educational culture.

Intellectual advancement should be unfettered by sectarianism, but the profound reverence I entertain for the Holy Scriptures leads me to express here the hope, that the educational development intended by this gift, should never antagonize, but be in harmony with the great fundamental principles of Christian truth contained in them.[14]

Swarthmore College. That the said corporation be authorized to establish and maintain a school and college for the purpose of imparting to persons of both sexes knowledge in the various branches of science, literature and the arts, and the Board of Managers shall have power to confer upon the graduates of the said College and upon others when by their proficiency in learning they may be entitled thereto, such degrees as are conferred by other colleges and universities in the United States.[15]

Most of these typical statements of institutional objectives reflect the social and cultural values of their authors—whether an individual or a group, public or private. Some sound reasonably contemporary, even though a century old, while others have the quaint ring of historicity. But Dartmouth is no longer devoted to "christianizing Children of Pagans," nor does Tulane limit itself to the education of "white young persons in the city of New Orleans"; the purposes embedded in founding documents are surely subject to modification. Indeed, the formulation of objectives of just about all of them are most general or even vague, so that if an institution is actually to carry them out, vastly more specific sets of goals need to be formulated. And since such delineating will inevitably take place at times that are progressively more future relative to the day of founding, the conditions and circumstances that prevail *then* must play a role in the specification of objectives. But because a charter grants certain powers and rights and the acceptance of those rights constitutes a promise to carry out the purposes for which they were given, it matters that those goals are specified and not altered arbitrarily, but in some way that is appropriate.

A homely analogy will make this clear. If I lend you my car so that you can drive your child to the doctor and the two of you drive to the baseball game instead, you've broken our little contract. In this simple case, an obvious way of legitimating so significant a change of destination is to ask my permission and receive it. To say the least, things are more complex in the institutional case, with the nature of an acceptable process to be looked at later on.[16] It might be worth noting here that a significant change of purposes is to be distinguished from going out of business altogether. For that is like not using the car at all, since none of the charter-granted rights or powers would henceforth be exercised.

The language of many founding documents may be general and vague, but it is not empty. On the one hand, the originating document specifies, in broad strokes, a set of functions the new institution is to fulfill. On the other, in varying language that appears again and again—some of it underlined in the excerpts cited above—the charter anchors the institution being founded in an ongoing tradition that has its roots in a quite distant past. A *college* or a *university* is being established that will resemble colleges and universities that already exist. This means, in the first instance, that in response to future conditions now unknown, the original institutional goals remain open to change, just as academic institutions founded in the past have evolved with changing times. But second, by tieing the new institution to ongoing practices and customs, it is destined to resemble existing colleges and universities in broader ways. Powers and rights are granted to the institution so as to give it a considerable measure of autonomy,[17] not only that it may fulfill its educational functions, but so that it is empowered to serve society in larger ways, in preserving, disseminating, and seeking knowledge and by engaging in discussion of social and cultural issues, thus subjecting current beliefs and practices to analysis and criticism. By not sitting in the middle of ongoing streams of politics and commerce, academic institutions are in a position to serve society by reflecting on the nature and directions of those currents.

Although we have made use of legal documents, our concern has been confined to their moral implications. A good thing, too, since it is very rare that a legal case is based on the charter of an institution, not to mention the founding document's statements regarding institutional objectives.[18] The state takes much more seriously, however, the momentous grant it makes to colleges and universities: their exemption from taxation. And you can't blame the law for caring. Think just of the sales taxes not paid by more than 3,700 IHEs that have budgets ranging from tens of millions to more than a billion dollars annually; think of the millions of acres their campuses occupy, many of them the finest chunks of real estate in their areas, all of them free of property tax. We are talking of a whopping forgone income on the part of several levels of government and of massive benefits to each and every IHE. Moreover, built into this institutional tax exemption is a powerful multiplier, since income taxes are reduced for those who make contributions to institutions that are tax exempt. Although we do not know just how much greater charitable giving is than it would be without this practice, no one doubts that the amounts are substantial; we certainly do know that wherever income tax is levied, these deductions constitute huge amounts of income relinquished by the collector. Through the Internal Revenue Code and the many analogous laws at other levels of government, society, in its American specification, puts its money where its mouth is.

That code provides that, "to be tax exempt, . . . the schools must like all 'charitable' organizations, meet all of the tax law requirements pertaining to these entities, including a showing that they are operated for public, rather than private, interests."[19] Specifically, Section 1.501(c)(3) "provides that an organization may be exempt from federal income tax if it is organized and operated exclusively for an 'educational' purpose."[20] In (3)(I) of that section, what is meant by "educational" is defined as being "related to instruction or training of the individual for the purpose of improving or developing his capabilities" or the "instruction of the public on subjects useful for the individual and beneficial to the community."[21]

If squabbles about charters seldom reach the courts, the Internal Revenue Service and the legal establishment are frequently concerned with the legitimacy of the tax exemption of an entire institution or of some of its activities. The issues vary considerably, though the concerns that underlie them are few. Most frequently, the courts are asked to determine whether some activity or practice of a college or university operates for private rather than public interest—anything from housing for college presidents to meals for students or research engaged in for some particular private purpose. Other issues of concern pertain to the scope of the public served: does the institution act for the benefit of *all* of the public or does it discriminate against some portions of it?[22] Less frequently, the courts have concerned themselves with the meaning of "education" and have tackled the distinction between education and propaganda, with only the former to be subsidized by society.[23]

And a subsidy it is. In a sense, the rights and powers granted in originating charters are creations ex nihilo, since they are gifts that essentially cost nothing to the giver. The immense benefits, however, that IHEs derive from their tax-exempt status are offset by losses to the taxing authority. In this manner, society, through its governmental agencies, contributes to the purchase, so to speak, of a set of activities for its members, its citizens: to educate, to preserve and increase the store of knowledge and to do so for the good of the public rather than for its own profit. Acceptance of the government's benefaction obligates the recipient institution to serve the public in appropriate ways; the assumption of the special status under discussion is tantamount to a promise to do that for which it is given.

We have not, to this point, distinguished between private and public IHEs; and with respect to the institutional obligation to fulfill its purposes this distinction makes no difference. In the first case, the desire to accomplish certain goals is imputed to the institution, with society responding by granting rights and financial advantages because it approves of those goals. Charter-granted powers and benefits derived from the tax laws then require the institution to do what it has proposed. In the second case, society, acting through some governmental agency, brings a college or university into existence because it wants its citizens educated and to be assured of the growth and preservation of knowledge. But because the *originating* desire to have certain goals achieved here resides in society rather than with the institution does not change the fact that benefits are conferred on it so that it can do that job. In both cases, the same obligation-creating bargain is struck: Benefits are conferred so as to enable the institution to do what it is meant to do.

But as we take cognizance of this private-public distinction, we are also reminded that tax exemption can hardly be the whole story about the financing of IHEs, since that pertains only to money they are *not* required to spend. To perform their functions, these institutions must have funds and these funds are given to it by private and public sources. To put it succinctly, colleges and universities operate with other people's money.*

Speaking of money, it will be worthwhile to stop a moment to convey an idea of the magnitude of the higher education establishment in the United States; it is formidable.** In the fall of 1995 there were 3,706 colleges and universities, of which 45 percent were public and 39 percent were two-year institutions [86 and 87]. These IHEs enrolled over 14 million students (10.02 million full-time equivalents), with public institutions educating 78 percent of these and 31 percent enrolled in two-year institutions [45 and 78]. And to minister to these students a lot of people are needed. In the fall of 1993, these 3,706 colleges and universities employed 2.6 million people (69 percent of them full time), including 915,500 faculty members (60 percent of them full time) and 143,600 mostly full-time administrators and managers of every sort [118]. That's more people than were working (in 1992 in all of the United States) in the manufacturing of every kind of food product, *combined* with all apparel and textile manufacturing employees (just under 2.5 million [739]); and there were more faculty members than the 626,000 people who worked in the entire paper and allied products industry [740].

---

*As has often been pointed out, public institutions that do not also receive funds from private sources are rare and the private institutions that are not the recipients, as well, of public monies are rarer still. That does not change the fact that colleges and universities spend other people's money.

**Education statistics are taken from Anderson, 1998, with the table number given in brackets; business statistics are taken from *Statistical Abstract*, 1997, with the page number indicated in brackets.

And when one looks at dollars, the numbers become truly staggering. Total higher education "industry" revenues in 1993–4 were $179.2 billion [94], which was substantially higher than the 1994 revenues of $153.8 billion that flowed into the entire U.S. communications industry, including every kind of broadcasting, publishing, recording, information services, advertising agencies, and more [565]. Of this total almost $49 billion came in the form of tuition and fees [94]—just a little less than the entire 1994 payroll of $53.9 billion of the insurance industry [509]—while $69 billion was spent by all levels of government [94]. And while past performance, as they say, is no guarantee of future performance, in just twenty-four years, total higher education revenue has risen by a factor of 8.3, tuition income has multiplied 11 times, and government spending 6.8 times what it was in 1969–70, measured in current dollars [94]. When we talk about spending other people's money, we are speaking of a lot of it—and it continues to go up.

In business corporations the owners spend their own money in the effort to make more money. If the business thrives, they derive an income; if it falters, they lose some or all of what they had invested. Only the smallest fraction of what it takes to operate a college or university, if anything at all, comes from individuals responsible for running it, such as members of a board of trustees. Virtually all financing comes in the form of allocations or grants from various governmental sources, as donations and legacies from private individuals, from foundations and corporations, or in the form of fees and tuition. A lot of other people; a lot of money! What obligations does this largesse generate?

Consider, first, a grant or donation for a specific purpose. In an important way, such a bestowal resembles a purchase. Normally, when you give money to buy an object or a service, the person who accepts the money is obligated to provide the item in question or perform the service. This is the most obvious instance where giving money encumbers the recipient with obligations, leaving undiscussed the many ways even such simple transactions can deviate from "normal." Similarly, when a private donation or a governmental allocation is made so as to erect a chemistry laboratory building, endow a chair in American history or ophthalmology, give scholarships to impecunious aspiring engineers, or renovate the weight room for the football squad, the institution's obligation is to deliver the goods. Still, these contracts are not purchases, for when the goods are delivered, nothing is given directly to the person who foots the bill. And because the donor neither selects nor receives what he or she has "purchased," the relationship of donor to what is done with the funds bestowed is not like that of buyer to the object bought.

This difference has implications for the obligations that are incurred by the institutions to which such funds are given. Buyers of merchandise are saddled with the consequences of their choices. Caveat emptor is the ancient warning that you inspect the wares you purchase before handing over your money, because if you do not get what you thought you were paying for, the responsibility is yours. The donor, however, is not the buyer; the institution that receives the contributed money is the surrogate buyer of that for which the donor designated his or her contribution. But the contributor is neither the recipient of the goods or services nor the one to inspect them upon arrival. While the buyer of a car takes it back to the dealer for remediation if it soon develops engine trouble, the donor is not in a position to demand redress if what the IHE gets or does is not what the donor intended.

I am certainly not pointing to the remoteness of the donors from the objects their contributions buy—to the secondhandedness of this kind of "purchasing"—in order to argue that benefactors should be more directly involved in the activities of the colleges and universities to which they contribute and, paradoxically, become part-time administrators. Instead, I draw the conclusion that as the donors' surrogate buyer, these institutions owe particular conscientiousness in the way they spend their contributors' money. By way of analogy, I am free to be careless in investing my money, but I am required to be most conscientious when I invest for a child who has inherited some money. If my inattentiveness extends to my ward, I should not be entrusted to tend to the welfare of minors. An institution that lacks conscientiousness when funds given to it for one or another purpose undermines the trust needed to be the recipient of such gifts. Caveat donor!

It is useful to look first at donations to IHEs for quite specific purposes, because here the business of spending other people's money is writ small enough to see. Looking at the funding of all of higher education, however, vastly more money is given to institutions without such specification. Mostly, donors or taxpayers simply provide *operating* funds, that is, the money needed if the university or college—or one of its divisions or programs—is to go about its business. We are back, in other words, to institutional purposes as they are understood at the time of the donation or allocation. Whatever they are, the acceptance of these funds obligates an IHE to perform these functions thus underwritten and to do so with the utmost conscientiousness.*

---

*A governmental unit allocating funds or a taxing authority exempting an institution from a levy must be assumed to be acting in behalf of the society that created it. Acceptance of funds or exemption thus also obligates the institution to treat the members of that society fairly, that is, nondiscriminatorily. What that means in practice can be specified only with the context in which an institution exercises its choices.

III. Tuition, Students, and the Institution

Two major sources of other people's money with which colleges and universities go about their business remain to be taken up: tuition from students and external funding for research by faculty members and their staffs. While in later chapters we will comment on the institutional involvement in the research activities of its faculty members,[24] we will first explore at some length the special relationship of students to the institution, with a view to arriving at an understanding of administrative obligations as based on this primary function of colleges and universities.

Not surprisingly, a student's paying tuition to the bursar can have more than one import. It may simply be the payment of a fee for a service to be rendered, no different in kind from the payment made to a barber for a haircut or to the repairman to repair a washing machine— except that the barber and repairman will wait for their fee until after the service has been performed. Three interrelated characteristics make such transactions relatively straightforward purchases of services. First, what is to be accomplished by the work to be done—what the outcome should be—can be stated both by vendor and customer relatively unambiguously, though that may include pointing to other heads or to pictures in the case of the barber. Second, there is a sense in which both participants in the transaction know what needs to be done, though of course the customer is unlikely to be able actually to do it. (If this claim is unclear or seems implausible, I trust that it will be somewhat clearer and more plausible when, in a moment, these simple services are contrasted with other types of cases.) Third, the customer is able to evaluate the results of the services that were performed and can do so, moreover, right after the work has been finished.

In a higher education setting tuition is seldom expended for so straightforward an acquisition, granted that vastly more complex purchases are also made in the commercial world. Often, getting one's car repaired is anything but simple; nor do I so clearly know what I am doing when I buy a new roof for my house. We return to these complications in the next chapter; it is useful to begin by contrasting the activities of higher education with that haircut or washing machine repair. A possible analogue to those simple cases is a course intended to teach its students the rudiments of a specific word-processing program (although that is a most dubious instance of higher education) or one that will teach a practicing radiologist to work with a specific new piece of apparatus (again, a kind of continuing education course that is also hardly typical of what is taught at colleges and universities). But both of them do resemble conventional services in the three ways just mentioned, in

that students have a fairly specific idea of what to expect in the course
and are able to evaluate what was accomplished. We are as close as we
get, in higher education, to having a student's tuition purchase a service.

But mostly, our simple-purchase criteria are not met in the world of
colleges and universities. Even when we are speaking of a student paying tuition for a single course, not many resemble those just mentioned.
Courses about Shakespeare's plays, about the law of contracts, about
the American Revolution can take numerous shapes. Among other
things, they can differ in the material and skills that are covered, what
is said about the material, the methods used to convey it, and what is
required of students. What actually takes place can differ so much that
courses with identical titles and even descriptions could be aiming to
bring about quite different pedagogic goals. Thus, when students decide
to take Jones's Shakespeare course or Professor Hausman's torts, they
know much less about what will happen next than in the above cases.
Put another way, much less of what a student experiences is a product
of his or her decision. Moreover, when it's all done, it is very difficult to
translate a subjective sense of satisfaction or dissatisfaction (when there
actually *is* a distinct effect of such a kind) into an objective assessment
of what was accomplished—not to mention in comparison with possible
other versions of the course actually taken. The difference between such
transactions and buying a pig in a poke is that one doesn't *have* to do
the latter, since it's easy enough to open the sack. If tuition, here, is still
the payment for the purchase of a service, it certainly is of a peculiar
sort.

But tuition as payment for single courses is itself not the norm at
IHEs. Most typically, tuition is paid for entire educational programs:
from those leading to bachelor's degrees, where the student's aim is to
acquire an undergraduate education, to postbaccalaureate, so-called
professional programs, leading to a multiplicity of degrees, such as law,
dentistry, library science, and many more, to programs aiming at doc-
torates in a large number of different fields. There is a great variety
here, but note that all such programs are composed of a multitude of
components, most of which are themselves complex.

Two things seem to be true of all such college and university programs. First, with respect to many program components, what students
do is prescribed for them by others; there is not even the pretense that
they are making choices. On the other hand, regarding numerous program components, a student must make selections, some of them from
among a very large number of alternatives, about none of which the student can come to know all that much. While there is one sense in which
many students—though by no means all—know what they want, that
object of desire tends to be so general that there always remains a sense

in which students do not know what they want. And as regards an assessment of an entire program, it is even less plausible, in advance of experiencing it, to expect students to know what it takes to become a good lawyer—not to mention what should go into a good undergraduate education—than it is for them to know what a good Shakespeare course should consist of. Nor is the time of graduation a good time for evaluating the pedagogic aspect of the years spent studying. It may take years to get a reliable sense of how good one's education has been, or indeed it may never become clear. Buying an education is very different from most anything else one might purchase.

Students, of course, spend tuition money so as to derive benefits from their university or college, so that we may say that they are owed benefits in return. But even these brief and very abstract descriptions of what tuition pays for are sufficient to draw two important conclusions that will receive fuller exploration in the next chapter. First, it is a distortion and not just an oversimplification of what goes on in the context of higher education to say that students are customers purchasing services, in the way I am the barber's and appliance repairman's customer. A measure of how great the distortion is our sense of inappropriateness if college graduates' dissatisfaction with their education simply is dismissed with the reminder that as buyers of their education they should have been more careful, as if nothing further needed to be said than blaming these students for negligence in shopping. Students, then, are not customers, but *clients*, persons *who employ the services of a professional*, as the dictionary puts it. The many and varied obligations—here only pointed to, but not specified—that are generated by the student-professional relationship can thus be collected under the general heading of *professional obligations*.* While we can note that these obligations will be included among those generated by the granting of a charter, tax-exempt status, and the allocation of funds (as taken up, above), no quick answer can be given about their nature. We already know that the rendering of a service for a fee paid is not an adequate analysis, but elaboration on this aspect of the client-professional relationship will be postponed to the next chapter.

What remains is to identify the professional who is "employed" by the student/client, leading to the second conclusion to be drawn from our discussion of what tuition pays for. That story is complicated and

---

*Although we are here concerned with the obligations of professionals, it must not be forgotten that, as clients, students have significant responsibilities of their own. Even—or especially—in an ideal professional setting, students are never passive recipients of an education, but learn only by themselves engaging in significant work.

will be taken up more fully in the next chapter; here we confine our-selves to the claim that in the first instance, the professional of whom students are the clients is the college or university as an institution.

And not merely because that is the name that goes on the tuition check. Consider the simplest possible case: the difference between studying the violin with a concert violinist at her 57th Street studio and taking lessons from a violinist at the Manhattan School of Music a few blocks away. There's no way of telling who would be the better teacher; it is even perfectly possible that the same teacher is available at both these venues. However, should there be complaints about the teacher, they would, in the first case, have to be lodged with the teacher herself; with whom else could one lodge a complaint? In the second case, if communicating with the teacher does not resolve the problem, the stu-dent appropriately turns to an administrator at the Manhattan School, since that institution in some sense warrants the teachers in its employ.

That's at the simple end of a continuum. Institutional involvement of students enrolled in degree programs is multitudinous, starting with the fact that degree requirements are corporately set. Undergraduate educa-tion as conducted at most colleges and universities most obviously in-volves many components of the institution, since students are engaged in a wide variety of campus activities, both inside and outside the class-room. One is thus inclined to say that tuition does not pay for a specified number of courses, but for participation in a program that may involve ministration by virtually the entire institution. Accordingly, although a student is attended to by many different professionals, it makes no sense to single out some part of an IHE or some person within it as *the* profes-sional of whom the student is the client. Instead, the institution itself is the professional of whom the student is the client.

Perhaps this linguistic awkwardness can be overcome by noting a close analogy to a hospital. After all, as a patient there, I am likely to receive the care first of this nurse, then of that doctor, followed by this nurse's aid, that dietician, this resident, that specialist joining my physi-cian, that other nurse, and so on. Such a sequence describes what hap-pens to me, people fussing over me, one at a time or in groups. But it would be wrong to conclude (I hope) that when I move (or am moved) from one professional to the next, I am subjected to discrete, unrelated ministrations, as they would be if one afternoon I first go to my ophthal-mologist to get my eyes checked and then to my dentist to have a tooth filled. Instead, I am in the care of the *hospital*, of an *institution* that has a way of assigning tasks to the many people needed to take care of me and organizes them so as to accomplish the complex job of attending to my illness.

In the light of such relationships, colleges and universities and hospitals are appropriately called *professional institutions*, with patients the clients of the latter and students (among others) the clients of the former.

The next chapter will explore what is involved in having an IHE be a professional institution; to bring to a conclusion the topic of this chapter, in the interim, we turn to summarize the sources of institutional obligations so far discussed. We noted, first, that whether an IHE is public or private, a governmental agency grants to it a set of rights and privileges in an originating charter, so as to enable it to carry out its purposes. The granting agency does so because it deems the IHE's purposes to contribute to the welfare of society. We can thus say that the institution owes to society that it carry out these purposes, however they may be transformed in the course of time. More specifically—because of a given type of tax law—governmental authorities grant to the institution and to donors to it exemption from the taxes that profit-making institutions are required to pay. Again, this valuable privilege is conferred because the purposes of the institution are regarded as beneficial to society and generate the responsibility that the IHE carry out its functions.

But IHEs spend other people's money in more direct ways. Private individuals and organizations or governmental agencies grant funds, so that an institution is enabled to carry out specified tasks and accomplish designated goals. More broadly, funds are consigned to colleges and universities so that they may operate their programs, few or many, that they may go about the business for which they exist. In accepting all of this money IHEs incur the obligation to perform the various functions that might be specified and to carry out their institutional purposes. They have the duty, furthermore, to engage in these activities with a heightened degree of conscientiousness.

Finally, we have seen that because IHEs undertake to educate students, they must be regarded as professional institutions, a fact that generates for them a large bundle of obligations. While not much has so far been said about these, we may take it for granted that these profession-related duties will subsume many of those engendered by the other means discussed.

Notes

1. Friedman, 1970.
2. Friedman, 1970, 153.
3. Friedman, 1970, 157.
4. A good sampling is the discussion in the second chapter of Bowie, 1982,

which agonizes but then only adds "respect for legitimate individual rights" to Friedman's obeisance to the laws and ethical norms as qualifying the essential corporate goal of "maximizing profits" (34).

5. Looking at these two business ethics anthologies will provide a good start: Beauchamp and Bowie, 1993, and Hoffman and Moore, 1990.

6. Evan and Freeman, 1993, 80.

7. Evan and Freeman, 1993, 79.

8. Evan and Freeman, 1993, 79.

9. Friedman, 1970, 153.

10. Elliott and Chambers, 1934, 179; capitalization and spelling as in the original.

11. Elliott and Chambers, 1934, 134.

12. Elliott and Chambers, 1934, 464–5.

13. Elliott and Chambers, 1934, 576.

14. Elliott and Chambers, 1934, 485.

15. Elliott and Chambers, 1934, 480–81.

16. See chapter 3, section II.

17. See De George, 1997, 8–13.

18. This statement rests on some informal consultation with knowledgeable members of the legal profession and on the fact that in a comprehensive book on the law of higher education of over 1,000 pages, the only evidence I could find of litigation involving the *purpose* of an IHE was a single case of a petition to incorporate a new institution. See Kaplin and Lee, 1995, 682–83.

19. Hopkins, 1992, 17; also see, below, Appendix 1, 127.

20. Hopkins, 1992, 177; also see, below, Appendix 1, 127.

21. Hopkins, 1992, 177; also see, below, Appendix 1, 127.

22. See Kaplin and Lee, 1995, 776–82, and Hopkins, 1992, 235, for examples.

23. See Hopkins, 1992, 193.

24. See chapter 5 and chapter 6, sections IV and V.

Chapter 2

Colleges and Universities as Professional Institutions

I. The Nature of Professions and the Relationship of Professionals to Their Clients

Changes in the nature of occupations and employment that began to accelerate earlier in this century led sociologists to make the study of professions and the process of professionalization an important part of their work. As social scientists, their goal is to describe distinctively professional behavior—medicine and law usually serve as paradigms—and to develop theories as to how the features and practices of professions come about. It would take us too far afield to delve extensively into this literature; but a brief look at this empirical work will show that it has moral implications relevant to our subject.

A fruitful beginning is to set down some of the characteristics of a profession; but first some provisos. To begin with, sociologists tend to regard one set of traits as essential and others as derivative—with the former "sociologically causal"[1] of the latter—but are not necessarily in agreement as to which is which.[2] Since there is broad agreement on a longer list of characteristics (of whatever sort) of a profession, this issue of causality will not affect our discussion. Second, no one believes there to be an absolute distinction between occupations that are professions and those that are not.[3] Accordingly, an occupation can be more or less professional and, given that professions are characterized by numerous traits, it can be (more or less) professional in these rather than those respects. Finally, just which occupations are meaningfully called professions changes over time. Some drop out—phrenology, for example, once was something of a profession, but is no longer—but, obviously, far more have been added since the beginning of this century and continue to be at an accelerating rate.

17

The first characteristic that makes an occupation a profession—following W. J. Goode, who makes but two traits essential to a definition—is that it requires "prolonged specialized training in a body of abstract knowledge."[4] Every profession calls for its own mix of theoretical and practical knowledge. Thus, the growth of knowledge in a particular domain can stimulate the progressive transformation of a craft into a profession: "barber" into dentist, trainer into physical therapist, to give two examples, with concomitant changes in the educational and training requirements of future members of the profession.*

The second essential trait of a profession is that it possesses "a collectivity or service orientation."[5] Professions engage in activities that society needs; the members of professions regard themselves first as persons engaged in serving these needs and as acting in their own interest only secondarily. Again, what society needs changes from one place or period to the next, prompted by a variety of stimuli. Included among these can be the success of the practitioners of a *business* in persuading the public that they are actually performing a *social service*. Thus, "[t]he insurance salesmen try to free themselves of the business label; they are not selling, they are giving people expert and objective diagnosis of their risks and advising them as to the best manner of protecting themselves."[6]** What a society needs, in short, is not determined by means of philosophical analysis, but is instead a function of what a significant portion of that society believes and feels and does, as well as on the state of knowledge.

Given this starting point of two essential characteristics of a profession, we are in the position to explore some of the relationships that obtain between a professional and a client. The professional has something the client needs: a problem to be solved, a condition to be alleviated, a goal to be reached. However, the form that this takes in the typical case does not limit what the professional does to some activity that is prescribed in some manual—in the way in which the service person repairs that washing machine, following the manufacturer's handbook. Rather,

---

*This framework, incidentally, helps us to understand why Plato considers physicians and shoemakers to be craftsmen on precisely the same plane, since in his day both occupations depended more or less equally on experience rather than on the theoretical knowledge that would have "elevated" the former to the status of profession.

**But aside from the aspirations of insurance salesmen to attain a higher status derived from the claim of performing a social service, it is credible to suppose that the instruments of insurance have or will become so complex and sophisticated that considerable knowledge is needed to make an informed insurance decision. If this fact also leads to more and more theoretical education of insurance specialists, that cadre would be launched on the road to becoming a profession.

it presupposes professional judgment as to what should be done and the ability to apply to particular cases a theory that has been studied. The professional, accordingly, is able to do things that a layperson is unable to do: perform a bypass operation, write a brief for an appellate court, build a bridge over a ravine. In addition, the professional comes close to having a monopoly on judgments as to what, in a given case, is the best thing to do: whether to do open-heart surgery and, if so, just what kind; whether to appeal to a higher court and, if so, just how; just where to place a bridge and what kind.

Thus, by virtue of the professional's long period of study and apprenticeship, there is a significant asymmetry in the relationship between professional and client. Moreover, this unevenness remains even in the exceptional case in which the client also possesses the relevant professional training. There is an old saying that a lawyer who represents himself has a fool for a client. Even with professional knowledge, "clients" cannot be expected to be able to maintain the requisite professional attitude of objectivity toward their own problems, a belief that is corroborated in medicine by the practice that physicians treat neither themselves nor their own families, but seek help from professional colleagues.

"A customer determines what services and/or commodities he wants, and he shops around until he finds them . . . [on] the premise that he has the capacity to appraise his own needs and to judge the potential of the service or commodity to satisfy them. . . . In a professional relationship, however, the professional dictates what is good or evil for the client, who has no choice but to accede to professional judgment."[7] Clients' lack of the knowledge and objectivity possessed by professionals gives them no choice but to *trust* the professional called in to solve a problem or attain a desired goal.

Because the professional-client relationship can be characterized in this way, it gives rise to discussions of paternalism, the practice modeled on parents, knowing better than their children, to decide courses of action for the children's good, even when they override the children's desires. In days of yore, behaving like a benevolent father vis-à-vis his child was held to be a good thing and seen as modeled after God's relationship to his creatures. That was also how kings and lords should behave toward their subjects, as well as priests toward their congregants and physicians toward their patients. The fatherly role was the model for the most respected ranks in society.

But, at least for us, a society shaped by the egalitarianism of the Enlightenment, the days in which such a hierarchical order is valued have long since gone. It is one thing to behave parentally toward children— minors—whose minds and wills have not yet reached the maturity that enables them to know what is in their best interest and to act on that knowledge. It is quite another to reduce adults to that position, since that compromises their autonomy as (adult) human beings and abridges their right to determine *themselves* what is best for them. Paternalism violates the dictum that all persons are created equal, giving no one the right to make decisions for another. Within this framework, "[w]e may define paternalism as the overriding or restricting of rights or freedoms of individuals for their own good."[8]

On this prevalent negative view of paternalism, every effort must be made to shape the relationship between professional and client in such a way that the autonomy of the latter is respected. The physician is not to be regarded as the kindly authority who acts in behalf of the patient, but as an advisor who acts only after the patient has given his or her informed consent. And because illness and injury and approaching death produce many different kinds of difficult situations for physician and patient, much has been written about ways in which the former can at all times respect the integrity of the person of the latter, without giving up on such goals as the minimizing of the patient's pain.[9]

Since the relationship between clients and professionals can be given a great variety of shapes, it is possible to push the principle of client autonomy very far, with the professional deferring to the client in all decisions pertaining to his or her case. But in many instances, this comes to a matter of neither having one's cake, nor eating it. On the one hand, the insistence on such strict autonomy might best be called consumerism, in that the client simply becomes a customer, acting "[on] the premise that he has the capacity to appraise his own needs and to judge the potential of the service or commodity to satisfy them."[10] But because that premise is often false, acting autonomously may precisely deprive one of a good many of those competencies of a professional that presumably led one to him or her in the first place.*

Yet on the other hand, even the most meticulous attention by the professional to the autonomy of clients cannot eliminate that fundamental inequality between them. Even assuming that, with consummate pedagogic skill, the expert explains to the layperson just what the alternative paths are and what their results can be expected to be, that language as used by the speaker where it is rooted in broad experience does not have the same meaning when it is heard by a novice. All this before consider-

---

*"Giving a patient the numerical probabilities of outcomes for different treatments, and then asking the patient to make a decision, is tantamount to abandoning the patient, [Edmund] Pellegrino said. An element of trust in the healing relationship is a recognition that the patient is dependent on the information and actions of the physician." ("Limitation of Autonomy," 1993, 8.)

ing that there is an element of art in all professions, so that not every-thing in the application of theory to particular cases can be articulated in the first place; all this before considering that clients may not be clear about their own preferences, especially in complex situations contain-ing many unknowns; and all that before considering that what is appre-hended is different for someone in need or even distress from how it is understood by someone "merely" pursuing his or her metier. In short, the substance of that "informed consent" need not at all live up to its form, so that even when every effort is made to preserve the autonomy of clients—at the distinct risk of reducing the professional's ability to benefit them—there remains an element of paternalism. What is finally done need not be in conflict with the client's desires—insofar as he or she is clear about them—but is nevertheless not fully a function of the client's decision.

It has been objected that the professional-client relationship we have been describing is not properly thought of as an instance of paternalism. Joan C. Callahan writes,

> In writing a brief, an attorney acts on the presumption that he knows what is best for his client; in bending the knees of her trainee in a certain way, the suburban golf pro acts on the presumption that she knows what is best for her pupil; in showing his apprentice how to use a lathe, the skilled cabi-netmaker acts on the presumption that he knows what is best for his nov-ice. Such actions fall under models other than that of the parent/child rela-tionship. The attorney acts as a fiduciary in behalf of his principal; the golf instructor and cabinetmaker act as masters passing on skills. . . . [C]entral to the relationships in our examples is the fact that the trained professional uses his or her skills to provide a service *requested* by the client or trainee.[11]

Whoever takes the issue of paternalism seriously will not be overly impressed by this argument. The fact that a particular relationship is re-quested will not bleach all paternalism out of the one that is subse-quently created, no more than would the fact that I sell myself into bondage willingly (*pace* John Locke) shields the resulting relationship from the charge that it is slavery. The question, after all, is neither about the voluntariness nor the benignity of the relationship—many congre-gants choose to put themselves into the hands of their clergy, and the latter may indeed have in focus the best interests of the former—but the nature of the relationship itself. Accordingly, we can disagree about the moral and psychological undesirability of paternalism—in general or in this kind of case or that—but not make it go away altogether by likening the relationship to the harmless one of hired golf pro to ambitious duffer.

One might distinguish different kinds and degrees of paternalism and in this way make the discussion of paternalism in the professional-client relationship considerably more extensive and complex. But such a discussion would here be a digression, since what matters for us is the *inequality* of professional and client that gives rise to the charge of paternalism in the first place. What matters is that this inequality prevents the characterization of the relationship between professional and client as a contract. Most simply put, "[f]rom the perspective of morality, parties to a contract are equals."[12] But "no gain results from treating as equals people who are not relevantly equal in fact or from assuming nonexisting freedoms."[13] The inequalities previously pointed to preclude the needed freedom to bargain as equals, with a view to arriving at the respective obligations of professional and client.

Moreover, most often it is antecedently not even known just what the professional is to do to earn the fee a contract might call for. By contrast, while we don't necessarily spell out just everything a cleaning service must do in someone's house so as to earn its fee, service and serviced can contract by exchanging a few words and by relying on a common, nonexpert knowledge of what it is to maintain a clean house. The same cannot be said when a lawyer is engaged to represent someone in a divorce or a physician to deal with an ailment. What they will do in their clients' behalf—and how—will be determined by their knowledge, both diagnostic and curative, and may very well change in the course of the time of the professional's service. What, then, should the contract be *about*?*

If the professional-client relationship is not contractual, the latter has no choice but to trust the former. We have noted that fact already: It is what the sociological observers of professions have said all along. "A central feature, then, of all professions, is the motto . . . *credat emptor* [buyer believe]. . . . The client is to trust the professional."[14] Not surprisingly, when one asks what is an *appropriate* relationship, the same conclusion is reached. It has been called *fiduciary* because "the client must rely on the professional to use his or her knowledge and ability in the client's interests," which leads to the normative implication that

---

*The point here being made is not contradicted by the existence of malpractice suits. The failure to live up to a contract is to fail to deliver the goods or services specified in the contract: a car that works, a house that's clean. Malpractice is linked only indirectly to the outcome of the professional's activity: Patients die, law cases are lost in spite of excellent performances by physicians and attorneys, respectively. Malpractice pertains to the *way* in which the professional acts: The patient died, the case was lost because physician, lawyer did their work *negligently, incompetently*—just what you don't expect from a professional.

"the professional has special obligations to the client to ensure that the trust and reliance are justified."[15]

The client trusts; the professional "asks to be trusted."[16] Professionals, therefore, have obligations toward their clients, of a general kind, such as conscientiousness in pursuit of the clients' interests,[17] as well as many that are specific to the various professions and to particular cases. But what, in the real world, makes it more rather than less likely that trusted professionals will be trustworthy? Remember, we are doing without a contract, that is, without specific mutual promises that spell out what the duties of each of the contracting parties are. Were there a contract, its terms would permit the determination of whether those duties were satisfactorily discharged—in principle, on the basis of evidence that is open to inspection by a third party, who, whether in a legal context or otherwise, would be in a position to adjudicate. What the real world has generated, instead, is a number of further—derivative—characteristics of professions that complement the clients' need to trust with mechanisms that tend to make professionals more trustworthy.

Three are prevalent and important. First, professions, organized as societies, develop codes of conduct that spell out, often in considerable detail, what appropriate professional behavior is—in law, medicine, nursing, social work, engineering, and many more.[18] Depending on the degree of professionalization, all or most practitioners are members of these organizations and participate directly or—more likely!—indirectly in the formulation of such codes. Second, most mature professions have the power to license those who wish to practice, requiring the fulfillment of conditions or the passing of examinations of varying degrees of elaborateness and stringency. Whatever the mechanism that leads to the attainment of a license to practice, many such systems of credentialing have the force of law. With licensing, then, society tends to grant a monopoly to the overseeing professional organization and obtains, in exchange, some measure of quality control over those permitted to practice. Third, training and apprenticeship undergone by budding professionals and subsequent participation in professional societies initiate and sustain its members in a profession's culture that profoundly affects their practitioners' behavior and beliefs—far beyond the technical requirements of professional practice.[19] Thus, if I am asked why I should trust professionals whom I engage to help me (aside from the fact that I don't have a choice), it is because of the processes that produced them and made them what they are and the processes that continue to control or influence them as they go about their business. Thus, instead of relying for control on the specificity of a contract to do this or deliver that, professions impinge on the *persons* who do the

doing and delivering, though we shall want to revisit the issue of the re-
liability of that dominion.[20]

A concluding note regarding the distinctions here made. No doubt
many of the statements above are excessively sweeping and the contrast
between the pairs, professional-client and vendor-customer, more
sharply drawn than is often found in the complicated marketplace of our
waning century. On one side, not all professional services are equally
complex nor is the need for professional services always accompanied
by stress. Even in situations that are very involved, we can envisage instances in which a professional-client relationship does meet the ethical
as well as the legal requirements of a contract: when, for example, a
corporation or other agency is represented by its own staff lawyers or
engineers to engage outside professionals—lawyers or engineers—to
perform a needed service. More interestingly—if only because so ubiq-
uitously—there is an inequality between vendor and consumer in the
purchasing of many a modern product of a highly advanced technology,
one that requires the buyer to place some trust in those who make and
sell what is purchased. The facts that underlie this situation have not
converted car salesmen or manufacturers of herbicides into professionals, but mechanisms have arisen that mimic or serve as substitutes for
the practices of professions. Governmental regulations pertaining to the
manufacture and labeling of a large range of products, the practice by
vendors of goods and services to issue guarantees and warranties, the
strengthening of product liability law in recent decades all serve to reduce those characteristics of products that the prudent buyer should be-
ware but usually is not in a position to. These concessions by theory to
the real world, however, do not much modify the relationship between
client and professional that has been depicted, with its central need for
the former to trust the latter.

II. Students as Clients of Institutions of Higher Education

Enough has been said about the nature of professions and of the relationship between their practitioners and clients to serve as background
for our exploration of the obligations of colleges and universities and
the people who staff their numerous posts. But, as was insisted in the
first chapter, it is with institutions themselves that we must begin. For
students, when they enroll in IHEs, are not simply entering an educational bazaar or academic shopping mall, however they may at times
think that's where they are. Colleges and universities are not just *places*
that house numbers of learned people peddling their pedagogic wares—
merely advantageous for students by locating many practitioners in

close proximity to each other, merely advantageous for practitioners by enabling them to share facilities, from libraries to cafeterias. Instead, the institutions themselves, colleges and universities, assume responsibilities of central significance.

Still confining ourselves to academic institutions in relation to their students, the required institutional tasks can conveniently be subsumed under five heads. First, the IHE gathers and maintains a *staff* of people who, together, are capable of educating its students in accord with the institution's mission. Second, each particular college and university provides the *support* needed to perform these educational functions— and they can be most elaborate—as well as give support, with personnel and facilities, to numerous activities one might collectively call para-academic. Third, while individual faculty members have considerable autonomy with respect to their teaching, the IHE determines corporately and at various organizational levels how the different educational programs it offers should be composed. In this way the institution impinges on individual faculty members' autonomy. Fourth, colleges and universities, as institutions, issue transcripts, certificates, diplomas, degrees, and licenses that *attest to the attainment* by a student of a certain type and level of educational achievement. Finally, each IHE not only engages faculty members, provides support, determines the shape of educational programs, and issues a variety of credentials, but warrants that persons, facilities, programs, and certifications indeed *fulfill their functions* and are what they propose to be.

These clusters of collaborative activities make the designation of IHEs as *professional* institutions most plausible. But given the fact that higher education is so patently a professional *product*—needed by society and rooted in extensive training, with clients (above all, students) having no choice but to trust the source from which they derive it—it is especially the fifth bundle of institutional functions that marks it as professional: the fact that the college or university vouches for the authenticity of its central activities.

Moreover, educational institutions are adorned by many of the trappings that are typical of professions. They participate in a variety of professional organizations, with the institutions themselves as members; some of these organizations have developed codes designed to regulate IHE behavior; and there are procedures for licensing colleges and universities, as well as some of their subdivisions, in the form of accreditation. All these accoutrements—which give credibility to the analogy between a professional person and a professional institution—play a role in generating professional obligations. Before we can turn to this topic, however, we must take a closer look at what it means for an institution to have obligations.

III. Institutions *Can* Have Obligations

Indeed, can an institution actually have obligations, can it be responsible for certain actions and be blameworthy when not performing them or when acting in ways incompatible with duties it has incurred? In short, should it be taken literally that institutions themselves can be moral agents, with all the implications of that fact? An affirmative answer is already foreshadowed in the fact that IHEs are created as legal entities—having their source, as we saw, in articles of incorporation granted by a state, when private, and in a state's constitution or legislation, when public. Thus, a college or university may own property, enter into contracts, sue and be sued; that is, as an institution, it is entitled to act in various ways and is legally responsible (and liable) for those actions; it has standing before the courts of the land. Indeed, an IHE is not merely *entitled* to act in diverse ways, but is *regarded* as doing so in all of its nooks and crannies, as can be seen in the immense variety of suits, successful and not, that have been brought against colleges and universities.[21]

The context for all this, however, is a given legal system, a framework of laws and practices that create what we call the legal *fiction* that institutions that have certain legal roots, so to speak, are persons, with all the characteristics that this legal system attributes to persons. However, if one proposes to attribute responsibility to an institution without relativizing this imputation to some set of laws, arguments are needed to show that this makes sense.

In a book called *Collective and Corporate Responsibility*,[22] Peter French has put forward reasons for holding that institutions as such can be responsible for certain actions. Indeed, he goes so far as to argue that corporations are persons—and not just in the eyes of the law. Although it is at best unclear whether his arguments entitle him to this full-strength conclusion, they do show that institutions can be moral agents, a thesis that is quite sufficient for our purposes. While French's concern is above all with the implication that corporations are therefore blameworthy, anything that is a moral agent is also capable of having duties and incurring obligations and, for that matter, can be praiseworthy for fulfilling them well.

French begins by distinguishing between two kinds of collectivity, aggregate and conglomerate, a distinction that will also be helpful when we take a closer look at academic institutions. The first kind of collectivity "is merely a collection of people. A change in an aggregate's membership will always entail a change in the identity of the collection. . . . By and large what is predicable of an aggregate collectivity is reducible to the assignment of like predication (allowing for some verbal leeway) to collectivity members."[23] The waiting room at the Greyhound bus station contains an aggregate collectivity. To say what that collectivity is doing is simply to take the sum of what all the individuals in that bunch are doing: sitting, standing, reading, talking, chewing gum, whatever detail we are interested in. Whenever people come and go, the collectivity changes—a little or a lot, depending on whether the additions and subtractions are few or many. All redheads in Minneapolis also constitute an aggregate collectivity, because, except for the traits that enable us to pick out this aggregate from all the stuff in the universe—that is, red hair on living humans in the place called Minneapolis—nothing is true of that totality except what is true of each of its components.

By contrast, "[a] conglomerate collectivity is an organization of individuals such that its identity is not exhausted by the conjunction of the identities of the persons in the organization. . . . A change in the specific persons associated in a conglomerate does not entail a corresponding change in the identity of the conglomerate. . . . [W]hat is predicable of a conglomerate is not necessarily predicable of all those or of any of those individuals associated with it, and this is also true of predications of responsibility."[24] Take the shoe store on the corner. It is making a lot of money, but that's certainly not true of everyone who works there; and it has been doing so ever since it was founded—before anyone now in it was even born.

Unlike aggregates, conglomerates are organized internally, so that different members play different roles within them, roles that prescribe a certain conduct (including exercising power over others) and proscribe other behavior. And because these roles persist, the identity of the conglomerate does not necessarily also change when persons who fill those roles are replaced by others.[25] Shoe salespersons come and go—one of them was actually fired for chewing gum on the job—but that shoe store remains the same.

The distinction between these two types of collectivity is not absolute; between a pure aggregate and a perfect conglomerate, we can find different kinds of intermediates, a fact that will have some bearing on our view of IHEs.* But before we can return to consider these institutions with which we are concerned, we need to show briefly how a collectivity, such as a corporation (French's paradigmatic conglomerate), can be said to be responsible for decisions/actions without having them

---

*French introduces his two types of collectivity as if he held the distinction between them to be sharp (1984, 5–18). But when he discusses a medical emergency team (120–128), he places the team as an intermediate between the two.

reducible to decisions/actions of individuals within it. Required are internal decision structures consisting of at least two elements: "(1) an organizational or responsibility flowchart that delineates stations and levels within the corporate power structure and (2) corporate-decision
recognition rule(s) (usually embedded in something called corporation
policy)."[26]

The institution's organizational scheme determines who is entitled to
make decisions about what and whether and how they need to be con-
firmed at another organizational level. The company's purchasing
agent, for example, is empowered to sign a contract to buy sheet steel,
assuming a request from the engineer in charge of manufacturing and
subject to approval by the financial officer. When these three people
have done those three things, the corporation has acted; the corporation
is the *cause* of the existence of that contract to buy steel. In such cases
the decision flowchart is likely to be unambiguous in the assignment of
functions: the head of human services is not authorized to sign such a
contract. Were that officer nevertheless to do so, one would not say that
the corporation contracted for that steel. It is worth remarking, however,
that one cannot count on having the organizational charts of all collectivities that are not mere aggregates assign roles to everyone and in
every way as expeditiously as that. This fact alone makes for intermedi-
aries between aggregates and (perfect) conglomerates.

But note, while it is just fine for the purchasing agent to buy tons of
steel, since it is needed in the manufacture of the company's products,
it is not fine for that officer to contract for the purchase of a truck full
of lollipops. Even if it had been recommended by a relevant functionary
and even if it were approved by the financial officer, the contract to buy
lollipops would not be an act of the corporation. This example is meant
to illustrate French's second condition, which requires that a corporate
act be subsumable under corporate policy. Providing raw material for
the factory's operations constitutes a corporate *reason* for buying steel.
The corporation, accordingly, not only *caused* the action in question,
but did so for a corporate *reason*—two conditions that are together sufficient for the assignment of moral responsibility.

Presumably, it is in no way this manufacturing company's policy to
stock up on vast supplies of candy, so that their purchase—by the purchasing agent, on the request of the engineer in charge of manufacturing, with the approval of the financial officer—must be taken to be the
result of a bizarre conspiracy of three individuals. In the absence of a
corporate reason for the act, the company cannot be held morally responsible.* But note that policies, too, need not be "complete," and

---

*That moral responsibility and legal liability are not the same is illustrated by apply to every act of every functionary in the organization, even taking it that everyone knows that much policy is implied, rather than explicitly stated in some document. This fact of incompleteness, again, allows for conglomerates that are less than perfect, but still by no means mere aggregates. Finally, just as the lollipops are not bought by the company, so the steel is not bought by the requesting engineer, the approving financial v.p., or even the purchasing agent who signed the contract. The acts of these individuals are, to use French's term, redescribable[27] as a corporate act. The steel is bought by the corporation and it is the corporation that must pay for the material shipped, not the people who participated in the process that led to the transaction.

Enough of shoes and steel and lollipops; let us return finally to colleges and universities. Small or large, with a mission that is sharply focused or one that bears the burden of a multiversity, virtually all IHEs possess an organizational structure and a set of policies that enable them to perform the kind of institutional functions that were earlier listed. Accordingly, the academic institution itself bears responsibility for gathering and maintaining a staff needed to carry out its mission; it is responsible for supporting those functions so that they can be carried out; it must determine, as an institution, what constitutes an education in this or that subject, at this or that level; it, the institution as such, "stands behind" the diplomas and certificates it issues; the college or university itself warrants that the functions required to be performed to carry out its mission are executed competently. Colleges and universities have obligations they acquire in the very articles that found them, that they incur by virtue of the privileges granted them by the state and of the funds that flow to them from public and private sources; above all, they incur obligations because they undertake to educate students and perform other functions that are beneficial to society.

The story of obligations can thus be seen as beginning with the obligations of an institution; but of course this is not where it ends. One possible delusion must be promptly dispelled: no person is automatically taken off the hook simply because moral responsibility is assigned to an institution. In French's words, "[t]he fact that their actions are redescribable as corporate actions and that corporate actions can be morally assessed is no shield from individual responsibility."[28] What individuals embedded in an institution actually do may not be the same

---

the fact that the corporation would surely owe the candy factory for those lollipops and perhaps even for steel delivered on the basis of a contract that was signed by the human services officer. As a corroboration of French's position here being adopted, the corporation is most likely to take the offending officials to court in either of those cases, for lacking the authority to do what they did.

action as that attributable to the institution, but, in the absence of magic, if there is to be an institutional act, individuals must do something. The registrar, for example, checks a student's transcript and, finding that all degree requirements have been fulfilled, prepares a certificate for the dean to sign. One person counts, the other one signs, but the institution certifies. In short, derived from the institutional obligations we have been speaking about are some of the most important obligations and duties of the administrators of colleges and universities. To these we now turn.

Notes

1. Goode, 1960, 903.
2. Four characteristics are singled out in Barber, 1963, 672; two in Goode, 1960, 903.
3. Goode, 1960, 903.
4. Goode, 1960, 903.
5. Goode, 1960, 903.
6. Hughes, 1963, 659.
7. Greenwood, 1957, 23.
8. Goldman, 1980, 161.
9. See, for example, the thoughtful discussion in Goldman, 1980, 161–229.
10. Greenwood, 1957, 23.
11. Callahan, 1986, 115–116; italics in original.
12. Bowie, 1982, 47.
13. Bayles, 1989, 72. Also see May, 1975, 35.
14. Hughes, 1963, 657; also see Goode, 1960, 904.
15. Bayles, 1989, 78. Also see "beneficence-in-trust" physician-patient model attributed to David C. Thomasma and Edmund Pellegrino, "Limitation of Autonomy," 1993, 6–8.
16. Hughes, 1963, 656.
17. Bayles, 1989, 79–99, discusses honesty, candor, competence, diligence, loyalty, fairness, and discretion as "obligations of trustworthiness," traits clearly relevant to the obligations of IHEs and administrators.
18. For examples, see Bayles, 1989, 103, fn33.
19. See, especially, Greenwood, 1957, 28–31.
20. See chapter 4.
21. For a revealing overview, one need only look at the index entry of "Liability" in Kaplin and Lee, 1995, 1013.
22. French, 1984.
23. French, 1984, 5.
24. French, 1984, 13.
25. French, 1984, 13–14.
26. French, 1984, 41.
27. French, 1984, e.g., 124.
28. French, 1944, 124.

Chapter 3

My Station and Its Duties

I. If Institutions of Higher Education Have Obligations, Their Administrators Do

The first chapter of this book concluded with the claim that IHEs have obligations by virtue of rights granted to them when they are created, so that they are enabled to perform certain educational and scholarly functions for society. Moreover, these rights are significantly extended by laws that exempt from taxation both the colleges and universities, as well as those who donate funds for their operation. And many do contribute; the public through allocations by all levels of government and private individuals and foundations by means of gifts and bequests gave more than $130 billion in 1993–4. By spending other people's money, IHEs incur obligations to fulfill the purposes of those donations. Finally and most importantly, funds are conveyed in the form of tuition from students—$49 billion that same year—a fact that led us, in the second chapter, to a characterization of colleges and universities as professional institutions that have obligations toward their clients.

As we now turn to those people whose actions are needed if institutions are to discharge their obligations, we must first posit a fundamental truth about IHEs that should never be lost sight of: by teaching and engaging in research, the professorate does the primary work of colleges and universities; the faculty and its students are the institutional sine qua non. Yet if one were to imagine these individuals to be left to themselves, each simply doing his or her own thing, we would indeed be visiting that academic bazaar. The picture may even seem idyllic: a school devoted entirely to teaching and learning. But not even the grove on the outskirts of Athens—the Academia that gave the academic enterprise its name—is likely to have conformed to that model. For surely Plato, probably without much consultation with his fellow teachers, decided on the students to be admitted to study in the Academia and pre-scribed the course of studies they were to follow. If so, his personal de-cisions were institutional decisions as well; his views as to what should be done were institutional policy. In French's language, Plato's author-ity converts a would-be aggregate of teachers and learners into a collec-tivity.

In the United States two and a half millennia later—if only because of the task of annually educating well over ten million students—it is unthinkable that one should be able to obtain a higher education at a pedagogic bazaar; nor is the model of the Academy plausible, with its single teacher/administrator. In modern times, an entire cadre of admin-istrators is necessary (if not always as many as there actually are!) for the conversion of an aggregate of teachers, learners, and various kinds of helpers into an institution of higher education. The divisibility of such a crowd of different folks into units that have specific, stable rela-tionships to each other is dependent on the existence of the administra-tors that head them and who then become the occupants of the boxes that make up the organizational charts familiar from faculty handbooks and institutional fact books. Administrators make possible that "respon-sibility flowchart"[1] that is needed if there is to be institutional responsi-bility and the accomplishment of institutional goals of the kind referred to earlier.

Now, a quick glance at the organizational chart of a college or univer-sity even of modest size will reveal that the term "administrator" refers to quite a variety of roles. For our purposes, however, it will be useful to distinguish two broad types: *instrumental* administrators and *academic* administrators. The distinction is serviceable, even though it must be acknowledged in advance that the boundary between them is not sharp, making it possible for there to be hybrids. All administrators are manag-ers of some kind, for

> [w]henever the achievement of some goal requires the activities of several or many persons, managers are needed to sequence and coordinate their operations, to ensure that required work is done properly, to correct errors and to cope with unforeseen incursions. Some people who are called *man-agers* in the secular world are called administrators on a campus. Thus while staff members do what it takes to register students and maintain a record of their grades, the registrar—the person who manages the depart-ment engaged in these operations—is numbered among campus adminis-trators. Similarly, a bursar is not unlike the manager of a department of ac-counts receivable in the world of business.[2]

Other administrators oversee everything from the maintenance of an in-stitution's buildings to that of its ledgers—with a variety of titles, all the way to vice president. Because this first administrative category consists of the managers of staff persons who—in many different ways, either directly or indirectly—*assist* faculty and students to carry out the institution's primary missions, we call them *instrumental* administrators.

Not surprisingly, our principal concern will be with the second category, namely, *academic* administrators, since it is they who are distinctive of IHEs. So classified are an institution's president, provost, and some of its vice presidents; it includes deans, of which there are several kinds that differ from each other organizationally; also in this category are the directors of such academic units as interdisciplinary centers and laboratories; belonging here are many, but not all, associates of the above, such as vice provosts and associate deans; finally and, as administrators, with a most ambiguous status, there are the chairpersons of academic departments. These various officials are called academic administrators, because their concerns are with an institution's academic missions, because they work with faculty and are concerned with the academic pursuits of students.

As a breed, academic administrators are sui generis. Nothing like it is to be found in the world of business, and while they have some resemblances to hospital administrators and perhaps to certain governmental roles, we would not gain much illumination by pursing these similarities. Of course academic administrators also have managerial responsibilities. At the very least, they manage their own offices. More often than not, in a world that is becoming ever more bureaucratic, they are burdened with a multitude of institutional "housekeeping" functions that must be considered to be managerial. But there is no single term or perspicuous phrase that conveys what their main activities are; that is why we were driven, in the previous paragraph, to such vague phrases as "work with faculty" and "concerned with students." For in no normal sense of the term do they *manage* groups of faculty members or students, in the way in which registrars manage the clerks, computer programmers, secretaries, etc. who work in their offices.[3] While they do make many decisions autonomously or together with other administrators, most of their most important ones are made in collaboration with their faculty or its representatives (and to a lesser extent with students), in ways that have no real analogue outside the academic world.

If the way in which academic administrators go about their business is difficult to describe in a few words, it is not at all mysterious what academic administrators are intended to accomplish. *For they are the assignees of central obligations incurred by the institutions they serve.* Their activities and decisions, as we said, must be such that their college or university "maintains a staff of people . . . capable of educating its students in accord with the institution's mission"; that their institution provides the support that is needed for its educational and para-academic functions; that their institution's educational (and para-academic) programs take the form appropriate to their purposes; that their college or university provides the documents, from transcripts to diplomas, "that attest to the attainment by a student of a certain type and level of educational achievement"; and that the implied institutional warrant that its activities are what they purport to be is justified.

The academic administrators of a college or university, in other words, are the *persons* who occupy the boxes in the organizational charts who make the decisions that enable their *institution* to discharge its obligations. In every properly organized IHE, moreover, instrumental administrators report, either directly or indirectly, to academic administrators, so that the determination of how the institution's functions are carried out remains in the hands of the latter. In fact, it is a part of what it means to have a properly organized IHE that its administrative relationships have such a design. Indeed, one might call it a metaduty of academic administrators to see to it that the institution is organized in a way suitable for the accomplishment of the goals to which it is committed.

But to the broad claim here made about administrators' duties, intending the full moral sense of that term, readers may be tempted to make the following kind of reply. To be sure, when people are hired to do a job, any job, they assume the obligation to do what they are hired and compensated for, provided what they are supposed to do is neither illegal nor immoral. Take the managers of some unit of Universal Motors. Other things being equal, whoever does a really good job will get raises and perhaps be promoted; whoever persists in performing poorly is likely to be fired or demoted. But a "normal" performance is just the one that is expected in the job and simply earns that check for the jobholder on payday. This "normal" performance constitutes the duty the unit manager is obliged to discharge, because it is contracted for when an agreement is made to do a given job for a specified wage. It may be praiseworthy to do more, but one would be hard put to make out the case that one has an *obligation* to do more. Why should the moral situation for an academic administrator be any different?

That is not a rhetorical question; it deserves an answer. Unlike business corporations, IHEs have been characterized as *professional* institutions that possess, as such, obligations that are not borne by the likes of Universal Motors. We are here confronted by the payoff of this fact for the people who conduct the affairs of colleges and universities. It would be deeply paradoxical to claim, on the one hand, that, as institutions, colleges and universities have complex sets of obligations, but, on the other, that no person functioning within them has duties that are directly (causally) related to having these institutional obligations discharged. Thus, to assume the role of administrator in an academic institution is to step into a moral context that is different from that which is entered when one becomes a manager in a business, just as being a member of a family constitutes a moral setting that is unlike that of being a member of a bowling club, independent of the specific role in family or club.

In response, it might be countered that while academic administrators are indeed required to act in ways that will ensure that the institution discharges its obligations, this assignment is given to these administrators in just the same way in which duties are assigned to Universal Motors managers. After all, because Universal Motors has a goal—to make money for its stockholders—the jobs its managers are to perform are described for them in ways that will further this goal; so let those managers simply do their jobs. Analogously, because IHEs are professional institutions with obligations of their own, let that fact be reflected in the job descriptions of its various levels of academic administration and let those administrators do the jobs assigned to them.

Two things are wrong with this reply. First, let's be clear that each manager at Universal Motors might be doing his or her assigned job, while the company nevertheless loses money and its stock goes down. It's too bad when that happens, because the stockholders now stand to lose money rather than gain it. Regretful, but not immoral. Investors buy stock where they have reason to hope that a company will do well, but there is no contract, explicit or implied, that an investment must yield a profit. But we have seen that the relationship between a college or university and the society that gives it a charter, its supporters and its clients, is very different. It would not just be regretful, but *wrong*, if at some IHE students were not learning anything (including those willing and able to discharge their responsibilities in the complex process of becoming educated); degrees were issued to people who hadn't earned them; contributions were accepted for programs that didn't exist—even if one could make out a sense in which academic administrators were doing the jobs assigned to them. But precisely because of this incoherence, there can be no such sense; academic administrators *are* the assignees of the duty to bring about their institution's goals, so that no description of their jobs would be complete if it failed to make appropriate reference to those institutional goals.*

---

*Clearly, we are not here considering the potential gap between administrators trying to bring about an institution's goals and succeeding in doing so. We cannot assign the duty to succeed, since that may depend on many things not under the control of the agent.

But second, it would in any case be naive to hold that one could devise job descriptions for managers at any level that amounted to a set of prescriptions, which, provided they are followed faithfully, would lead to the accomplishment of the desired job. If, in Fritz Lang's *Metropolis*, the conversion of factory workers into rule-following automata is a fantasy that is dramatically effective, an analogous scene for managers has the potential of being hilariously comic. The more complex the managerial position or the higher up on an organizational chart, the less plausible it is that one could reduce to rules what is there to be done. It has proven very possible indeed to have a computer play world-class chess without having that device understand the strategies that lead to an opponent's being checkmated. Such programs rely on a vast memory bank of possible moves and their consequences and on the computer's ability to "consider" (search through) them in the required time. Human beings do not possess these capacities; they must play chess by being aware of goals that must be pursued in the different phases of a game and of the game's ultimate goal. Similarly, for corporate managers and academic administrators to be able to do their jobs, both types must understand and be guided not only by the goals their own units are intended to bring about, but by some grasp of the goals of the larger organization of which they are a part. To managers of both kinds, in other words, the responsibility of striving to bring about the goals of the institutions in which they function is in various ways assigned. But, again, while this fact has no moral import for the managers of Universal Motors, it emphatically does for administrators of IHEs.*

Since the moral implications for academic administrators derive from the fact that IHEs are professional institutions, it would seem plausible—perhaps even necessary—to regard academic administrators as members of a profession as well. Not so; forever a protoprofession, perhaps, but not a full-fledged profession, since at least one essential characteristic is missing: extensive systematic instruction, both theoretical and practical, characteristic of such paradigmatic professions as medicine and law. Neither the fact that there exists a "professional" organization of academic administrators nor the fact that the vast majority of people who wind up in academic administration do have some extensive training turns out to be sufficient reason to overcome that obstacle.

---

*Given the conclusion we reached in this paragraph, we avoid a puzzle that would have to be solved if one supposed that all managerial jobs were describable in terms of rules alone. For were that so, one would need to answer the question as to who makes sure—and how—those many prescriptions for all those jobs are designed in such a way that following is likely to bring about the institution's goals. How, in other words, would institutional goals become the goals of particular people?

There is an American Association of University Administrators, and it formulates a code as its *Mission Statement and Professional Standards*. That mission statement, however, is primarily concerned with the welfare of administrators, rather than with providing directions for how they are to minister to their clients. And on the topic we have just been discussing their code gets it exactly wrong. "An Administrator has the responsibility" it declares, "to perform the duties of his or her office as defined in the written statement of the terms of employment, or as defined in an official handbook of the institution."[5] (A sentence that means to imply, I suspect, that what is not explicitly so prescribed cannot be a responsibility.) Professions are indeed adorned with codes; but this code of the organization of university administrators is not sufficient to dignify its membership as a profession. Indeed, academic administration is profession-*like* in part precisely because its roles cannot be encompassed by the kind of contract here proposed, even if here and there such "terms of employment" describe a part of an administrator's role.

The matter of training is more complex. Very few persons become academic administrators without having at some prior time completed an extensive and arduous educational program. But that educational regimen most likely led to an advanced degree in a specific field—perhaps a Ph.D. in a science or humanistic field or a professional degree such as an M.D. or M.B.A. If professionals are produced by these programs, they are physicists or geologists, art historians or students of French literature, cardiologists or specialists in marketing. The degree attained is not in academic administration, though that is the would-be profession we are talking about. To be sure, there is a handful of programs leading to degrees in administration, but few of their graduates are selected for higher administrative posts and least of all by prestigious institutions. The vast majority of persons holding academic administrative posts are then professionals in other subjects, but not in academic administration.

This reality reflects paradoxical but deep-seated principles about the functioning of the academy that will concern us in a variety of ways. But the upshot here is that in an important respect academic administration does fall short of being a profession. Nevertheless, administrators cannot escape the fact that they must see to it that the obligations of their institutions are discharged: obligations to its students and other clients, as well as obligations of those IHEs to their profession—that of higher education. It is not far-fetched to call academic administration a vocation or a calling, terms that do catch the obligation-generating aspects of a profession. Indeed, in one respect, some of the most important responsibilities of an administrator resemble a clergyman's pastoral duty to visit the sick and the bereaved. Given the mission of (most) clergy, comforting those who are in this way deprived is part of the job of priests or rabbis, making members of the clergy remiss (that is, negligent of their duties) if they refrain from that activity, even if no one ever told them to perform these functions. And so with the obligations of the academic administrator. The ends toward which academic administrators should strive—and they *should* strive toward these ends—are directly rooted in the singularities of the enterprise of higher education and in the specificities of particular academic institutions.

We might paraphrase F. H. Bradley and, substituting "administrator" for "individual," note that an academic administrator, apart from his or her community—that is, the administrator's institution—is merely an abstraction. "What he has to do depends on what his place is, what his function is and that all comes from his station in the organism," that is, from the role in that institution. "What is it then that [he or she] is to realize? We have said it in 'my station and its duties.' "[6] *Au fond*, Bradley still needs a metaphysical foundation to be able to claim that performing one's functions in state and community serves the requirements of morality. By contrast, the obligation to carry out the duties that academic administrators derive from the goals of their institutions is founded on the very conditions of the existence of those institutions. To be sure, those conditions are empirical ("merely" so, Bradley might interject), but they become the antecedents of complex hypothetical imperatives of the form: "since the institution is committed to x-ing, the dean ought to do y."

II. Institutional Goals and Administrative Obligations

Earlier (in chapter 1 and repeated in this chapter), I spoke of a number of broad administrative functions—such as maintaining and supporting a staff of people to educate an IHE's students—that were predicated on that institution's mission. A consideration of these goals raises two types of question, neither of them susceptible to a succinct response. The first, to be considered here, concerns the substantive selection of educational and para-educational programs; just what constraints are there on decisions as to what an institution should aim to do and, more generally, what are administrative obligations vis-à-vis the determination and articulation of an institution's mission? The second cluster of questions, to be taken up in the next two chapters, pertains to the manner in which a college or university goes about its business, or, more pointedly, to the quality with which it executes those programs. Although the consideration of the moral dimensions of neither of these themes lends itself to tight arguments and briskly formulated conclusions, it would be a serious omission to deliberate solely about means, while treating ends as if they were untouchably ordained by the heavens.

The particular goals of a college or university are of course specific to each institution, and in one way they are first set down in a founding charter or legislation. But, as we have seen,[7] by and large these statements of institutional purposes are not of much help as guides to action, since most of them are so general or vague (or both) as to point at best in a general direction. But even if such founding statements of institutional purposes had the requisite precision and specificity, they could hardly serve as institutional signposts in perpetuity. Times change, we say, and that in many respects; and for a century now at an ever-accelerating pace. It is thus unthinkable that the mission of an IHE could stay fixed, assuming its "generic" goal to remain that of providing higher education to a population, near or far away or both. We saw that provided the tax code is not violated, the law allows an institution to specify or change an institutional mission virtually without limitation. As long as a college or university doesn't start making a profit and its pedagogy doesn't transmute into indoctrination, there is not likely to be a legal (or tax code) bar to having an IHE change or add or subtract any program it might choose, in whatever way it decides. Thus the question to be raised is what moral constraints, if any, are relevant to such choices of mission.

The question is relevant here, since the academic administrators of an institution should have—and usually do—a significant voice in the formulation of the goals of an institution, even though those goals are normally set by its governing board (whose role falls outside the scope of this book). Wherever a particular impetus for a change in goals may originate—in the faculty, the administration, or the board of an institution—it is certainly the role of the administration of a college or university, working with its faculty in various ways, to translate broadly stated goals into specific workable programs. But the fact that an IHE's board has the final say on institutional goals (as, in principle, on most everything else) does not relegate its administration to just minding the shop. First of all, the members of a board—laypersons who devote only a fraction of their time to that role—are dependent on advice and guidance from those who know their institution intimately and on a continuous basis. But "advice and guidance" does not say enough. Its board of directors would not expect to be able to govern Universal Motors without a chief executive officer; similarly, a board of trustees cannot administer a college or university without an analogous supervisor. If a board is responsible for the direction an institution takes, so is its chief administrator, with whatever advice and guidance that officer receives in turn from faculty and other administrators within the institution. It is not as paradoxical as it sounds to say that *both* board and CEO are *wholly* responsible for the objectives that a corporation or a university pursues. For, clearly, where both cannot agree on that direction, they must part company. Accordingly, the matter of moral limitations on the selection of institutional goals is a topic that must be pursued here.

In one sense, there probably are no moral constraints worth discussing. For there is not likely to be a specification or transformation of institutional goals that cannot be justified by *some* set of circumstances, assuming broad limits, such as those set by the tax code and by such obvious restrictions that there should be no programs that are themselves immoral, say, in advanced shoplifting. If, then, we are unlikely to learn much from considering, in general, what types of institutional goals ought or ought not to be adopted, it will be more fruitful to take up the moral appropriateness of the functioning of some precepts and principles in the determination and justification of a change in institutional mission.

One principle is obvious. In the course of time, circumstances may change in such a way that operating the educational programs for which an institution was founded no longer serves the broader purposes, explicitly stated or implied, they were intended to serve—such as being of use to some segment of society. In such a case, an institution is justified in dropping and adding programs, in order to fulfill such broader original purposes under altered conditions. A program in mining engineering, for example, may have been created to serve the population of the region, because it furnished expertise needed by its industry. Mining is no longer done here, but electronic parts are being increasingly manufactured instead. Mounting a new program in electrical engineering would then be justified by the stated or unstated institutional goal of making the population of the region economically viable.

Indeed, other things being equal, that a program is needed (in the community served by the IHE, including the nation or the entire globe) is a reason to establish it. But that ceteris paribus includes quite a package of reservations. Yes, establish the program because it is needed—provided it attains a certain level of quality (a subject to which we will return later). Yes, mount the program—provided that doing so does not undermine central functions of the institution, by swallowing essential resources, for example. It is of course perfectly permissible to make the decision to eliminate or reduce functions that had previously been central, for a variety of good reasons. What this reservation stipulates is that programmatic changes not lead to the starving of existing functions, without making a considered decision to reduce them, but that changes are made, instead, in a haze of institutional self-deception that there is any such deprivation at all.

Yet a larger issue is raised when we talk about "needed" programs, because that context has, in recent years, led many a college and university to give marketing considerations an inappropriate place in their educational operations. "If we establish this program or modify that one, we can attract more students to the institution—or perhaps more students who pay full tuition—because there is a market out there." Or, "With this program modification we can enroll better football players, assuring us of a better season on the playing field." There are confusions here, and they are morally relevant.

The second of these proposals may seem more obviously wrong, though many an alumnus will never be persuaded of that. Nevertheless, their widespread popularity notwithstanding, collegiate athletics are *subsidiary* to the institution's educational functions—if only because there would be collegiate education without collegiate athletics, but not the latter without the former. The creation or modification of an educational program, accordingly, the sole merit of which is its service to spectator sports, converts a professional educational institution into a quasi-professional athletic one, with education subsidiary thereto. Nothing changes if the team's record is to be improved for the sake of increasing donations to the institution. For even assuming, dubiously, that greater athletic success will actually do that, the institutional mission is being undermined. A college or university exists to fulfill certain purposes, and it raises funds so as to be able to pursue these objectives or to do so more effectively. If, instead, an educational program is instituted for the sake of increasing support, a central institutional end has been reduced to a means, while means have been elevated to the status of end.

A reader may concede that athletics should not be put ahead of education, but be quite puzzled that I object to having an institution determine what the market wants and then devise educational programs that meet known student demand. To clarify, a distinction needs to be drawn, even though—or precisely because—the differences to be pointed to are not always perceived, by practitioners or even observers. Of course it is the job of educational institutions to identify educational needs, worldwide, national, or local, and to set about developing courses and programs that meet those needs. Speaking schematically, this means that relevant members of colleges and universities first determine that if society's tasks are to be accomplished, including those of science and scholarship, there will have to be people who possess certain clusters of knowledge and abilities and proceed, second, to devise or modify educational programs that will, in their professional judgment, meet those needs and do so in ways appropriate to higher education. Those programs are then available to students who envisage playing the pertinent roles in the future. Other things being equal, where large numbers of students identify the same social roles for which an IHE has developed a program, there will be a good market for those educational services.

This stance contrasts sharply, if often invisibly, with a considerably crasser marketing outlook. When its language means in the educational context what it means in the business world, the institution attempts to find out what potential students *want* and then goes ahead to devise courses and programs that supply just what is wanted. That's what fast-food restaurants do, and the ones that do it well make big bucks. Potential students are regarded as potential consumers; they are not persons with needs that require professional attention, but people with desires they want fulfilled. The institution then aims to provide what it believes the students it seeks to attract want, largely unmitigated by educational judgment or by the standards of higher education that prevail elsewhere in the institution or did so at other times. The demand of some set of students may thus be met, but the institution that goes about it in this way becomes just another vendor in the marketplace and, in effect, abdicates its professional role by shifting the responsibility for making central educational decisions to the students.

The issue is "simply" that of the integrity of the institution as educational, as professional. Those scare quotes are quite appropriate, because the topic under discussion is a particularly fertile source of hypocrisy and sophistry. Academics are at least as susceptible to self-deception as the rest of humankind, and, because many of them are clever people, they are often good at it. In institutional discussions and decision-making processes, respectable, even high-minded, justificatory reasons and arguments may well hide—from the speakers themselves and not just the listeners—that what gives shape to a course or program or brings it into existence is the objective of fulfilling perceived student desires rather than the educators' response to a societal pedagogic need. The perspicuousness of such curricular discussions is not advanced by the fact that many a market-driven program of dubious educational value not only finds customers, but has them profess their satisfaction with what is offered. (It is best not to ask whether that satisfaction derives from new knowledge and skills acquired or from credits or degree attained, that is, certification with its value in the marketplace.) But the fact that in some circumstances exploitation is mutual does not raise the moral level of the interaction.

For institutions, as for persons, integrity is harder to maintain in bad times than in good, when the shrinking of alternative courses of action increases the temptation to transgress, bolstered by the fact that bad times increase the capacity for self-deception. It is therefore worthwhile to look at the situation when for a particular IHE times are so bad that it has only the choice of becoming wholly market-driven (in the present sense) or cease to exist. To stay alive, the college shapes all of its curricula to whatever is wanted in its corner of the world, vigilantly staying abreast of changing student desires. What remains is a reductio ad absurdum of an IHE. The tuition of students pays for services rendered: The institution's form remains that of a college society, while its substance has become a business.

So the place doesn't make a profit and return money to investors; but then neither does many a neighborhood restaurant or grocery store, where all the money that comes in is used to enable mom and pop and a few employees to be fed, clothed, and housed and perhaps accorded a vacation now and then. Such an establishment does not, therefore, become a "not-for-profit" institution, since that distinction does not only rest on the absence of profit, but on the kind of services it performs. But where an IHE serves its market in the way in which the neighborhood convenience store does, the lack of a return on investment surely does not warrant its having a special status, one that distinguishes it from other establishments—the myriad businesses of the world—all serving their markets in the best ways they can.

What is a perfectly reasonable way to keep mom and pop going nullifies the professional character of an educational institution. The institution that has been described is no longer capable of meeting its professional obligations to its clients and therefore does not meet its obligations to its profession.* And just as surgeons who have become unable (say, because of arthritis) to wield a scalpel with the skill needed to operate competently owe it to their profession (and not just to potential patients) to cease to undertake operations, so IHEs are obligated by *their* profession to cease to exist as such, rather than be de facto transformed into vendors. Hara-kiri is the honorable solution: institutional suicide, after dependents are taken care of in the best way that circumstances permit.

---

*The federal appeals court for the District of Columbia agreed with an accrediting agency that being a for-profit institution was sufficient reason for the agency to refuse to consider an IHE for accreditation—that is, to be a member of good standing in its profession. (See Kaplin and Lee, 1995, 876 and 881.) There the intent to make a profit constitutes a presumption that the services rendered are driven by the market, as is the case in other "for-profit" institutions. If so, it is surely only because the courts do not wish to get into the business of making qualitative judgments about the workings of academic institutions and the education they provide that nonprofit-making, mom-and-pop colleges retain their formal status as tax-exempt institutions. No, doubt, too, such cases are not brought to the attention of the courts in the first place.

We have moved from selecting the goals of colleges and universities to having institutions do away with themselves, but have been virtually silent about the obligations of administrators. Given the station as it has been described, what are the duties of academic administrators; what are they to *do*? One is tempted to reply with a flood of practical advice—let the president do this, the provost act in that way, and have the dean pursue the following path, with the reader no doubt appreciating such a descent from our lofty perch of abstraction. But however practical, such prescriptions would certainly not constitute moral obligations. After all, IHEs differ from each other in numerous ways, including in the ways they are organized. And although one may have sundry opinions, and strong ones,[8] as to better and worse forms of organization, it would be the height of hubris to claim that all such views are propelled by moral force. But there is at least one obligation, central to our present topic, that academic administrators at all levels must discharge, a duty that constitutes a significant part of their leadership role, an administrative function that must be added to those reviewed at the beginning of this chapter. It is the job of academic administrators to articulate with some specificity the academic and para-academic goals of the institution and to initiate and oversee the processes that modify and change those goals.

It is important that academic administrators see to it that the members of IHEs maintain an awareness of the IHEs' goals, because the nature of these institutions and of the persons who inhabit them are such that awareness cannot be counted on as a matter of course. To begin with, two institutional characteristics make for considerable centrifugality, of a kind seldom to be found in business corporations. First, while IHEs vary considerably in their complexity, the organization of just about all of them can only be called loose. Although faculty members are organized into groups—departments, schools, centers—they do not "report" to the administrators who head those groups, as do employees of a corporation to the managers of their units. While that's a long story, suffice it to say here that administrators do not assign tasks to faculty members with a specificity that is usually taken for granted in the business world, nor do they supervise and evaluate their execution in ways that are normal in most other places of work. One result of such an attenuated form of oversight makes for a diminished level of communication within a college or university, not only "vertically" (between faculty member and unit head), but also "horizontally," that is, among faculty members—even within a unit and emphatically across departmental and school boundaries.

The second trait of any college or university that accounts for centrifugality is the fact that not only does the institution itself pursue a multiplicity of goals that are at best loosely related to each other, but the same individual may be engaged in several such quite disparate tasks. Thus, a single faculty member may be teaching composition to freshmen, writing a book on the Norse sources of *Beowulf,* and advising premedical students on their academic careers. It is easy, when so occupied, to lose track of the relationship between one's own activities and the larger whole of which they are a part—and doubly so for the kind of temperament that is attracted to the academic metier. For the very traits that characterize the best faculty members, such as concentration and zeal, also have a tendency to obscure for them the forest in favor of the trees. Without reminders as to what is individual and what is corporate, instructors can come to lose sight, for example, of the relationship of a course to an educational program of which it is a part, reminders that are contained in the articulation of institutional goals.

This is a sensible suggestion, a reader might concede, perhaps even good advice for academic administrators; but how is it distinguished from other administrative moves that might be recommended; why should it be held to be a moral obligation to follow it? A response to this question requires us to recall again that IHEs are professional institutions and to examine how their obligations are assigned to those who function within them. To put it bluntly, the way in which these *institutions* are professional, no *individual* within them is professional. It is obvious that an institution—or some significant subdivision of it, but not just this or that professor—provides students with a liberal arts education (with a selection of concentrations), a medical education, a business education, and many more. But it is also true that there are no professional designers of such programs, determining what they are to be composed of, since there is no professional liberal arts educator (or liberal arts-in-economics educator), no professional medicine educator, no professional business educator, and so on. That is as it should be; it boggles the mind to try to imagine the education such professional educators would need to have. But this fact makes designing educational programs a *collective* task of various members of an IHE, calling on individuals with different academic specialities and skills—in which they *are* professionals—to act together to determine the make-up of a liberal arts education in economics, of the education of a medical doctor, a mechanical engineer, etc.

It must be determined who the relevant people are to perform such tasks; they must be organized in a way that enables them to deliberate and act—in effect, be a component in an academic responsibility flowchart. The leading role in this crucial institutional task belongs to academic administrators, even though they may themselves make only few or no substantive contributions to the outcome, to the programs being fashioned. Administrators must see to it that the assignments to be carried out are adequately formulated; indeed, that they are formulated in the first place. To them belongs the job of assuring that an appropriate team is harnessed to the task and that the task is performed in a responsible way.*

An administrator so engaged might be thought of as performing a kind of operation bootstrap or as a magician pulling a rabbit out of a hat. For these administrative ministrations direct the process in which the deliberations of nonprofessional individuals (considered as educators) lead to institutional decisions that *are* professional. The professional nature of colleges and universities is in the care of their academic administrators, and that makes them above all the keepers of their institutional missions. Necessary components of this duty are the articulation of what the institution aims to achieve, so as to keep these objectives before the entire community, and the initiation and guidance of the processes that lead to changes in these goals. In the next chapter we will begin to explore the obligations of administrators with respect to the activities aimed at bringing about these goals.

Notes

1. French, 1984, 41.
2. Weingartner, 1996, xv; italics in original. The present discussion is based on pp. xiv–xviii of that book.
3. Scc Weingartner, 1996, xvi.
4. See Weingartner, 1996, xvii–xviii.
5. AAUA, 1994, 2(b).
6. Bradley, 1927, 173, including the quotations.
7. In chapter 1, section II.
8. For mine, see Weingartner, 1996, *passim.*

---

*This glance at central administrative tasks gives some indication why academic administrators are largely academics in one or another field who have turned to administration, rather than persons with degrees in administration. These leadership functions—not to mention those of supervision to be taken up in chapter 6—presuppose a real understanding of academic activities and genuine familiarity with the kinds of persons who engage in them. They require, furthermore, that the administrator gain the respect of the faculty that is to be led, a difficult feat at best for anyone who can be regarded as intending to boss such independent creatures as faculty members. It is of course not impossible that all this can be achieved by someone whose education and career is in administration; success is only much more likely for fellow academics. Although the analogy clearly has its limits, it is much more probable that effective field generals have risen through the ranks as officers in a functioning army, rather than as students and teachers of strategy and tactics in a war college.

Chapter 4

Quality: Teaching

I. The Competent Institution

Where it is appropriate for clients to trust an institution, that institution must at the least be competent. This holds for academic institutions as it does for medical ones. To be sure, the latter profession treats conditions that are usually acute, painful, and manifestly disabling, if not downright life-threatening, while the ignorance to be dispelled by education is painlessly chronic, incapacitating in much more obscure ways, and very seldom fatal. There is thus no need for emergency wards and operating rooms in colleges and universities. But the fact that there is a difference between how it *feels* to be ignorant or unskilled and being sick or injured does not change the fact that both patients and students are clients who must be treated competently by the professionals who minister to them.

As earlier mentioned, in the United States the professional nature of IHEs is recognized by the practice of institutional accreditation of colleges and universities. Accreditation by the appropriate regional commission—there are six of them—is the institutional analogue to the licensing of individual professionals to practice their metier, such as medicine or engineering. "Accreditation is the means of self-regulation and peer review adopted by the educational community."[1] "Through [their] evaluation activities, . . . the [a]ssociation[s] provide . . . public assurance about the educational quality of those schools and colleges that seek or wish to maintain membership, which is synonymous with accreditation."[2] Like the organizations of individual professionals, an important aim of accrediting associations is to help safeguard the autonomy of IHEs: "The accrediting process is intended to strengthen and sustain the quality and integrity of higher education, making it worthy of public confidence and minimizing the scope of external control."[3]

The commissions that actually do the work manage an elaborate process that determines whether or not a given institution merits to gain or retain accreditation. This procedure, however, presupposes that a "theoretical" job has been accomplished, namely the formulation of standards by means of which the accreditation worthiness of an institution can be measured. No doubt, some might want to add to such desiderata, formulate some of them differently, or even drop one or another of them as diversionary; nevertheless, a look at an example of a set of such criteria will bring us as close as we are likely to get to a general statement of a competent IHE and hence of the range of responsibilities of administrators of IHEs:*

1. [I]ntegrity in the institution's conduct of all its activities through humane and equitable policies dealing with students, faculty, staff, and other constituencies;
2. clearly stated mission and goals appropriate to the institution's resources and the needs of its constituencies;
3. clearly stated admissions and other student policies appropriate to the mission, goals, programs, and resources of the institution;
4. student services appropriate to the educational, personal, and career needs of the students;
5. faculty whose professional qualifications are appropriate to the mission and programs of the institution, who are committed to intellectual and professional development, and who form an adequate core to support the programs offered;
6. programs and courses which develop general intellectual skills such as the ability to form independent judgment, to weigh values, to understand fundamental theory, and to interact effectively in a culturally diverse world;
7. curricula which provide, emphasize, or rest upon education in the arts and sciences, even when they are attuned to professional or occupational requirements;
8. library/learning resources and services sufficient to support the programs offered and evidence of their use;
9. policies and procedures, qualitative and quantitative, as appropriate, which lead to the effective assessment of institutional, program, and student learning outcomes;
10. ongoing institutional self-study and planning aimed at increasing the institution's effectiveness;

---

*The statements of the several commissions are similar, but of course not identical. Because for our purposes succinctness is a virtue, what is cited here are the summary statements of the Middle States Association's "Characteristics of Excellence in Higher Education" (MSA, 1994, 4–5; numbering added).

11. financial resources sufficient to assure the quality and continuity of the institution's programs and services;
12. organization, administration, and governance which facilitate teaching, research, and learning and which foster their improvement within a framework of academic freedom;
13. a governing board actively fulfilling its responsibilities of policy and resource development;
14. physical facilities that meet the needs of the institution's programs and functions;
15. honesty and accuracy in published materials and in public and media relations;
16. responsiveness to the need for institutional change and renewal appropriate to institutional mission, goals, and resources.

Think of this set of statements as constituting a word picture of a competent academic institution, providing considerably more detail than the bare-bones list of institutional tasks given earlier. Students and society are served well by colleges and universities that possess these characteristics just outlined. But it is not through miracles that they come to have them. In direct and indirect ways the fact that institutions must acquire and retain these traits generates duties for academic administrators. Some of them have already been taken up, such as the formulation and articulation of institutional goals (nos. 2, 6, 7, and 16). Others, however, such as appropriate admissions practices and student services (nos. 3 and 4), require discussions of detail that would take us too far afield in a book that tries to look at academic administrations broadly.* Because so many activities that bring about the characteristics of a competent academic institution—indeed, most of them—are carried out by others than administrators, an entire chapter (chapter 6) will be devoted to issues stemming from administrators' roles as supervisors.

Teaching and research, however, as the two leading functions of IHEs, are not appropriately dealt with under more general headings. Academic administrators, moreover, have significant responsibilities if their institutions are to do well in the performance of these central activities. Accordingly, we take up in this chapter issues that pertain to teaching, while reserving a discussion of research for the next.

II. Teaching: Overcoming the Paradox

The faculty does the teaching, not, except incidentally, members of the administration. Nevertheless, in a variety of ways, academic administra-

---

*This is precisely the purpose served by several of the other volumes in this series on Issues in Academic Ethics. See, for example, the volume on student life on campus (Hoekema, 1994).

tors are responsible for how that teaching happens; indeed, they have a greater role and more significant obligations in that domain than is conventionally thought. But what magnifies their task is the fact that as agents for IHEs, they are confronted by yet another paradox of professionalism. As a norm, the faculties of colleges and universities are composed of professionals whose education—the training and degree that confers on them membership in a profession—is in a field of inquiry, a subject matter. Yet at IHEs an important part of what these PhDs, MDs, MBAs, LLDs, etc. are engaged to do is teach. (Indeed, often such teaching is not limited to the specific subject matter in which the instructors received their education, such as in general education courses.) For the activity of teaching itself, however, these academics are likely to have had little or no preparation. Although it is as teachers that the members of the faculty discharge one of the primary functions of the professional institution that employs them, they are not, as teachers, professionals at all.

For a long time, the academic establishment was in denial. "There is no paradox," it might have been said, "because what you need to know to be a good teacher of a particular subject is that subject—and that's all you need to know. At the level of higher education, teaching, as such, is not a professional activity." It was recognized that, indeed, some people are better at teaching than others, but that is so either just because they have a greater competency in their field or because they make a greater effort to teach well. When it was conceded that, though equally competent and conscientious, some people nevertheless are better teachers than others, the fact was attributed to differences in personality. Conveniently, one's personality is a product of nature and whatever nurture gives shape to character and temperament; it is not the result of schooling. Accordingly, there was nothing to be learned about teaching.

For a long time, there was little impetus to go beyond this lazy view of teaching; in a bygone era of undergraduate education, there seemed little need to be concerned with its quality. A caricature of those days of yore, simplifying and exaggerating, suggests that those who went to college were either members of a meritocracy or of a plutocracy. For the latter, college served less an economic than a socializing function. For them, the combination of a not-so-able student and mediocre teaching was simply redeemed by finding "the gentleman's C" to be quite satisfactory. For the former, undergraduate education was very much needed to get ahead in life; but for them, strong motivation and superior ability to learn were able to compensate, where needed, for professorial inadequacies. In neither case was there much urgency to think about teaching.

But during the third quarter of the twentieth century, those good old days were rapidly waning, and by the last quarter, they were gone. Beginning with the veterans of World War II, a vastly larger and more heterogeneous population came to participate in undergraduate education. Of necessity—a statistical necessity—the explosive expansion of the college population also meant that the number, if not necessarily proportion, of less qualified and less motivated students would increase as well, as would the number *and* proportion of those for whom success or failure in their studies would have significant economic consequences. Because, compared with an earlier, more elitist period, a much larger number of students were at risk of not benefitting sufficiently from their years in college, and because that made much more of a difference to the lives of far more people, the academy began to recognize that teaching mattered.

To be sure, that dawn of recognition is rising only slowly; full daylight has yet to be reached. The codes of ethics of some academic associations pay obeisance to the relevance of teaching to their work, but often merely as a fleeting curtsy. The "Statement on Professional Ethics of the American Association of University Professors" limits itself to the ringing declaration that "As members of an academic institution, professors seek above all to be effective teachers and scholars."[4] Other statements issued by the AAUP importantly stress that instructors' presentations should be relevant to the subject of the course and fair to different points of view, and they urge respect for students' opinions and fairness in their evaluations.[5] But there is no suggestion that the point of teaching is that students learn, that effectiveness of teaching is a complex and difficult matter.

Perusal of a small sample of codes of ethics of learned societies—in effect the associations of professionals as organized by field of inquiry—shows that most of them also enjoin their members to be proficient teachers. More extensive discussions, however, tend to be limited to the avoidance of a variety of wrongs, such as "the persistent intrusion of material unrelated to the subject of the course,"[6] imposing partisan views,[7] failing to acknowledge student collaborators,[8] and sometimes include quite elaborate prescriptions and proscriptions to assure that students are treated fairly.[9] The statement of responsibilities of law professors goes a bit further by including such specific directives as this one: "[Law professors] should prepare conscientiously for class and employ teaching methods appropriate for the subject matters and objectives of their courses."[10] In their 1997 *Code of Ethics,* the sociologists actually do *not* assume that one learns to teach en passant: "Sociologists conscientiously perform their teaching responsibilities. They have appropriate skills and knowledge or *are receiving appropriate training.*"[11]

But even if the codes of academic professions were to show more concern with teaching, what difference would that make? While some codes are intended to serve solely as guides to professional behavior, others do include mechanisms for their enforcement. Yet, if all of them did, what difference would *that* make in the real world? Even the influence on good practice of our paradigmatic professions of medicine and law is severely limited; notoriously, their associations typically fail to revoke the licenses of patently incompetent practitioners.[12] The very collegial nature of a profession—not to mention the diffidence of Americans to "snitch" and report to some authority the transgressions of others—weighs against the likelihood that professional codes of ethics are actually enforced. And as to our subject, it is so enormously difficult to envisage having cases of incompetent teaching taken to the ethics committee of a learned society and dealt with by the committee members that one might regard this as a reductio ad absurdum of professional self-regulation.

If the profession cannot act, the responsibility to do so shifts to the institution. "In the enforcement of ethical standards," says the "Statement on Professional Ethics of the American Association of University Professors," "the academic profession differs from those of law and medicine, whose associations act to ensure the integrity of members engaged in private practice [*sic*]. In the academic profession the individual institution of higher learning provides this assurance and so should normally handle questions concerning propriety of conduct within its own framework."[13]

That sentence concludes, "by reference to a faculty committee." Yet if that is intended to take care of such matters, this directive is also made problematical by the otherwise desirable trait of collegiality. Just as the AAUP overestimates the effectiveness of self-regulation of the professions of law and medicine, so does this statement underestimate the barriers to self-discipline within institutions. And if it is difficult for one colleague to accuse another of such rare and flagrant transgressions as plagiarism or falsification of data, faculty self-policing with respect to so widespread a misdeed as poor teaching is even less likely to happen. In any case, most academics are smart enough to avoid the accusation of being pots who call the kettle black.

This gives to academic administrators the primary responsibility for seeing to it that their institution's students are taught well. But when one recalls that an important—though not the sole—cause of inadequate teaching is that paradox of professionalism, it becomes clear that disciplining the faculty is not at all the first administrative task needed to bring about that goal. Just as it is inappropriate to punish a child for walking around with dangling shoelaces, if the child has never been taught to tie them, so it is futile to penalize faculty members for doing poorly what they have neither learned to do well, nor are supported in doing on a day-to-day basis.

But what *is* that first task? Should it not be to steer the process that brings new faculty to campus in such a way that the person who is engaged—for now assumed to be one of the most numerous kind of "new hire," namely a beginning faculty member—is a fine teacher? After all, for quite a few years now it has largely been a buyer's market—a situation not likely to change in the foreseeable future—one that gives colleges and universities the opportunity to select the kind of faculty they want: let 'em pick good teachers!

No doubt it is relevant advice to attend to a candidate's potential as a teacher,* but to leave it simply at "let 'em pick good teachers" makes one of two assumptions, neither of which is likely to be true. The first holds wrongly that not much needs to be learned about teaching, and the other supposes, improbably, that what needs to be learned about teaching was learned elsewhere, as part of a candidate's graduate education.

But if our envisioned candidate did not learn much about teaching in his or her path to the doctorate, *should* that not have been so? Should the argument not be made (or repeated!) that since graduate departments and professional schools of American universities are the main educators of the faculty of the colleges and universities of this country, they should finish the job and educate teachers, as well as practitioners of a field of inquiry or profession? Let there be no paradox of professionalism in the first place, in that doctoral or professional degrees are awarded to persons who have become professionals in their fields them *and* in the teaching of them.

It is certainly a good thing to have graduate departments pay more attention to pedagogy—if only because at most universities doctoral students do a considerable amount of undergraduate teaching. At the very least, teaching graduate students should be adequately guided and supervised in their teaching activities and by persons interested in and knowledgeable about pedagogical issues in the student teacher's field. But there are a number of reasons why educational programs at the postbaccalaureate level are not the right place for the job that needs doing. In the first place, while in some fields most (though not all) graduates aspire to become college teachers, in others career goals and ac-

---

*One of the projects of the American Association of Higher Education's teaching initiative pertains to the "pedagogical colloquium" and other ways of assessing teaching ability and potential when faculty candidates are being considered by a hiring institution. (See Hutchings, 1996, 107–109, and, below, Appendix 5 [C], 159, as well as Hutchings, 1997.)

tual paths are much more varied, and in professional schools only a very small fraction of persons receiving the degree become engaged in higher education. To require a serious teaching program would thus be unfair to those who have no intention of teaching and would surely be quietly thwarted (or noisily, depending on the era) by a significant proportion of students. On the other hand, an unserious program is not good enough.

Second, the object of graduate and professional education is to gain mastery of a complex field of study and to acquire the intellectual skills associated with it. It is right that advanced students be fully immersed in their subject matter and that their instructors be unfettered in demanding rigorous study in depth and breadth. Given such justified demands, it is unreasonable to insist that students serve an apprenticeship in two professions at once and probably futile if one were seriously to try to do so. And for reasons such as these, the actual efforts that are made in graduate programs to prepare for teaching tend to be perfunctory. The attention paid to teaching that is thus required of graduate students is largely a by-product of the need to have them earn their keep by teaching or is designed to dress up the résumés of graduates in search of scarce teaching positions. On the other hand, the serious efforts that are here and there made to launch students toward becoming professionals as teachers are mostly—and appropriately—voluntary and thus reach only a fraction of those who wind up as instructors in IHEs. In short, the job would never be done right, were one to insist that all those who come to teach in a college or university should be prepared to do so as part of their graduate education. One ought thus not insist.

Finally, and most importantly, it must be stressed that just as competence in a subject matter is not maintained without constant study and inquiry, so proficiency in teaching is not acquired once and for all, but requires ongoing attention. Thus, even if it were possible to do more as part of graduate education than is here supposed, it would not do to place the entire burden of ensuring good teaching in higher education on the graduate programs of our universities. Nor must one ignore, as we have been temporarily, the large population of less than exemplary instructors who are long past graduate study.

That brings us back to the institutions to which the graduates of postbaccalaureate programs are brought as beginning faculty members and where persons of all ranks are engaged in instructing students at all levels of postsecondary study. Very well, one might interject, the focus is on the institution where the teaching takes place, but why is this entire discussion embedded in a study of the obligations of academic administrators? Given that teaching is either an important or the most important function of faculty members—since that is what they are employed to do—why should those administrators not simply demand, as a condition of employment, that faculty members take steps "on the job" to overcome that paradox of professionalism—and be done with it? Let 'em learn to teach well; that's what they are paid for!

One truth here is undeniable: it is those who do the teaching who must learn to do it well; no one can do that for them. But everything else about such a brisk administrative *fiat lux* is thoroughly misleading. To begin with, many a faculty member would be surprised to hear that one of the highest concerns of the academic administrators who signed the papers that put him or her on the payroll was the education of the institution's students and that the new faculty member had been appointed to teach well. And if that thought had actually been expressed, that voicing may well have been indistinguishable from a ritual genuflection. Nothing much is likely to change a year and more later. More often than not, when salary increases and promotions are considered, those ceremonial bows in the direction of teaching continue, with few consequences in the real world. Nothing in such a story convinces faculty members that the quality of their teaching matters to their careers, especially as compared with other demands made of them, such as producing publications. There *is* a job here for academic administrators.

But to assure that good teaching is convincingly posited as an institutional priority and that the structure of rewards is brought into harmony with that fact is only part of what is needed. For these measures only provide motives for overcoming the paradox of professionalism, but do nothing to help instructors to act on them. For in the bleak places I am describing—I wish they were exceptional—instructors are left to themselves to determine what good teaching is, often guided only by the results of student evaluations—and that without counsel on how to interpret those questionnaires. No doubt such surveys can be informative,* but even assuming that the evaluation is very well done, good teaching is conceptualized in most of these instruments in a way that has been handed down from one uninformed and unreflective faculty generation to another, focusing on teaching as faculty performance. Moreover and mostly quite unintentionally, student evaluation—especially if it is the only evaluation of teaching—induces precisely the kind of consumeristic attitude that this book is taking such pains to assail, both on the parts

---

*W. J. McKeachie, perhaps the leading researcher in this field, in an article written with Matthew Kaplan, cites several studies that "attest to the validity of student ratings well beyond that of other sources of evidence about teaching" (McKeachie and Kaplan, 1996, 7). Nevertheless, it is tricky to get clear about just what is evaluated when teaching is evaluated. And when that question is broached, one's confidence in such a judgment is certainly shaken. See the discussion and references in Cahn, 1994, 38–54.

of "faculty-vendors" and "student-customers." I will never forget
when an outstanding and very smart assistant professor related to me
that when his chairperson told him that at promotion time he would
need good student evaluations to present to the dean, he changed his
teaching style and much improved his ratings. He also told me that he
thought that the students learned considerably less under the new dispensation. He wasn't cynical or outraged, just wry.

If teaching is to be treated with fitting seriousness, its end must be regarded to be students learning, with faculty "performance" one of the
means. And that requires establishing alternative methods of evaluation;
methods, moreover, that consciously aim at the improvement of teaching—and therefore of students learning—rather than at merely providing data for personnel decisions. (That the same instrument of student
evaluation of teaching can effectively serve both of these very different
purposes is a convenient illusion.) The regular and broad involvement
of the faculty is thus required, in the form of different kinds of peer review of teaching. If teaching is important, it merits the evaluative activities of faculty members, just as it is unquestioned that the results of faculty research activities are assessed by faculty associates.

This is not the place to give detailed advice as to how such reviewing
might be accomplished, but it is important to dispel the notion that there
is a sharp contrast in the evaluation of faculty research and teaching,
with the former easy (which it isn't—a matter to be taken up) and the
latter well-nigh impossible (which is equally false). While there is a
growing literature on this topic, the products of the Teaching Initiative
of the American Association for Higher Education are a convenient
source of reference for us.[14] Much can be accomplished by means of re-
ciprocal visits to classrooms and making a number of uses of the observations that are there made, including regular discussions of teaching,[15]
the maintaining of teaching portfolios,[16] or even a review of teaching by
members of other institutions.[17]

All of these methods of evaluation of teaching by faculty colleagues
can play their parts in such decisions as the determination of merit salary increases or promotion in rank, especially that which confers tenure.
But unlike simple questionnaires designed for such purposes and filled
out by students, these evaluative methods involving other faculty members can serve as the basis of advice about and assistance in teaching
that is specific to the subject matter and level in question. And that is
what is needed. It will not do to leave individual faculty members to
their own devices, hoping that they can and will do what it takes to become and remain truly effective teachers. Again, different chapters of
Making Teaching Community Property point to a variety of ways of
making teaching a communal concern for the faculty: "Teaching Cir-

cles: Starting the Conversation," "Mentoring: Teachers Teaching Other Teachers," "A Focus on Student Learning," "Team Teaching and Teaching Teams," "Collaborative Inquiry and Pedagogical Scholarship," and "Departmental Occasions for Collaboration."[18]

The faculty will have to do all of these things; but few of them will happen and none will be sustained for any length of time without administrative initiative, organizational efforts, and, not least, allocation of resources. If a "culture of teaching" (to use the felicitous phrase of the American Association for Higher Education's Teaching Initiative) is to become established on a campus, it will take much administrative leadership and support.[19]

Everything that has so far been said about the improvement of teaching might be regarded as a kind of extracurricular activity for faculty members in which they polish their techniques, while leaving unaffected the familiar framework in which most college teaching takes place: lecture courses with discussion or problem sessions; three weekly "contact hours"; competition among students rather than collaboration; and the size of classes a function of student demand, the size of the institution's budget, and the capacity of its classrooms. But superior pedagogy not only calls for the opportunity to experiment, but may require changes in any and all of these hallowed practices. If so, administrative imagination—not an oxymoron, I hope—is needed to replace the old bureaucratic ways, from the way courses are scheduled, to the way space is utilized, from the way students' progress toward graduation is measured (will they still earn credits?), to the way faculty members' teaching duties are determined.

Furthermore, genuine improvement of teaching is not like pouring old wine into new bottles. When the success of pedagogy is directly related to the degree to which students learn, it may well turn out that *what* is taught must also be reconsidered. For example, while there certainly is a place for survey courses, serious questions should surely be raised about just what a student learns in a course that is a manifestation of the widespread professorial obsession to "cover," in a semester, immense chunks of a subject. If the learning of students were measured by what they still know a year later—not to mention at graduation time and beyond—it may be that they learn next to nothing in those elaborate surveys presented in almost all fields. In short, significant coupling of teaching with learning has radical implications not only for the *way* in which institutions of higher education go about their business, but *for what that business is.*

Finally, more conventional administrative tasks are also needed to establish that "culture of teaching." We have noted that when candidates are considered for appointment, the teaching potentiality of these possible future faculty members must be carefully assessed, both to help the appointing institution make informed decisions and to impress upon candidates how seriously teaching is there taken. And we have insisted that the efforts and abilities of faculty members in that regard must have an effect on salary, continuance in the job, and rank. But the importance of teaching need not be stressed at the expense of research (in institutions where that is an important responsibility of faculty members); in the way the reverse is often true. But where both are demanded, certain practical consequences must be drawn, a vital and difficult administrative function. Above all, a context must be created that provides the opportunity for a candidate for tenure or promotion to succeed in both. Time is the indispensable ingredient here, so that a supportive institution will either require less teaching in the earlier years or extend the probationary period (*pace* AAUP) to give candidates enough time to learn to teach well and to put in sufficient time actually do so, *and* have the time needed to undertake the kind of scholarly activity that will demonstrate whether they measure up to the standards of the institution.

The more one reflects on the many aspects of an institution that must be configured so as to support effective teaching on an ongoing basis, the more one realizes how far so many institutions have drifted from devotion to this so central part of their mission. Earlier, we gave a number of practical reasons why it cannot be left to graduate education, on the one hand, and astute faculty appointment policies, on the other, to ensure that faculty members are effective teachers. But we must finally recognize that these reasons are ancillary to the moral dictate that places the responsibility for seeing to it that students are well served squarely on the shoulders of the institution whose students they are. Academic administrators must first achieve a heightened awareness of that mission, together with the understanding that it is their obligation to work at accomplishing it. Not to do so is a dereliction of duty.

III. Informed Consent

Before turning, in the next chapter, to administrative responsibilities with respect to faculty research, we must turn to an activity that is akin to teaching, the importance of which is most often underestimated. It was earlier argued that there is an irreducible asymmetry in the relationship between professionals (or professional institutions) and their clients.[20] That gap between knowing professional and relatively unenlightened client remains, even when serious efforts are made to bridge it. That this should be so is regretful in an essentially egalitarian society in which individual autonomy is highly—and rightly—prized. Informed consent by the client, accordingly, is vastly better than blind obedience to the expert, though even *that* concurrence still rests in part on trust. In the medical world, informed consent may take the form of repeated conferences of physicians with patients and family members, detailed and unhurried, with most questions addressed in such a way that the patients achieve the sense of genuine participation in decisions that affect their futures. Alas, "informed consent" can also be—and often is—a short ritual that leaves the patient in ignorance and confusion that is suffused with fear, but arms the physician with a signed piece of paper attesting to the "fact" that his or her duties to inform have been discharged.

The situation in the academy is similar. The fear is largely missing; the student's condition is not acute, as is the illness of the patient. But, with or without self-awareness on the student's part, there is ignorance and confusion wherever the choice of a course or educational program is not truly informed. The closest analogue to the medical situation is the institution's prescription of a requirement and the student's fulfilling it. Informed consent to pursuing the prescribed path means understanding what that requirement is and why it is imposed. That understanding matters, as it does in the medical situation, because it restores a measure of autonomy to the person who is acting in ways decreed by others. But in education, it plays an important additional role. Learning is not something that happens to one, the way a bypass operation does or the effects of a course of antibiotics. Students are participants in their education to a vastly greater extent than patients are in their healing, a participation that is not fostered by ignorance and confusion about what and why this curricular path.

Then there is a somewhat more distant analogue of informed consent that is more important still.[21] We speak of the *offerings* of a college or university; we say these offerings constitute educational *opportunities*. With respect to most of these, students are permitted to choose freely, so that they themselves determine to what educational path they consent. But these terms, "choose," "freely," "consent," constitute empty rhetoric, unless the choice is informed. Offerings are opportunities only if those who make the selections know what they are doing. Perhaps it would be healthy if fear *were* associated with these choices, as it is with the selection of a course of therapy, since educational choices, once made and acted on, are doubly irreversible. First, the experience of taking a course permanently changes the person taking it. If that does not always happen in the way originally envisaged either by student or teacher, there is no returning to the state prior to the educational encounter. Second, given the way the world works, what is later recognized as having been a mistaken choice can only seldom be rectified by taking the route that is subsequently seen as the correct one. And even when that is possible and the decision is in a manner of speaking reversed, the time and energy and resources expended on the mistaken direction are gone forever. For education to be effective, therefore, to ensure that what is possible for students—particularly undergraduates—becomes actual, academic institutions must provide a kind of paraeducation, an education about how to become educated. Without it, benefitting from the available educational opportunities is a matter of luck.

And there is much to learn. To begin with, there is the mundane matter of understanding what the courses that might be chosen are actually about. The very language of course titles, descriptions, and academic fields themselves is in effect a technical language that is acquired only fragmentarily, at best, without prolonged residence in the world of higher education. Courses, moreover, are not discrete entities, like beads on a string. Part of what they are derives from their relationship to other courses and to the intellectual world to which they belong. Novices need assistance to understand and guidance to make wise choices. Further, courses and course sequences stand in various relationships to the world of work and the professions, to future careers. Depending on how these relationships are perceived by a student, one educational path is taken and another is shunned. Yet those perceptions are often wrong, at times wildly so. Costly mistakes are thus made, because students act on the basis of beliefs that are, so to speak, picked up on the street. That this should be so in an IHE is surely wrong!

Finally, knowing what educational path to take presupposes not only knowledge of what routes there are that might be followed, but also knowledge of oneself—one's interests and predilections and the abilities one has to pursue them. A mature person can be counted on to have such self-knowledge; indeed, having it is a part of what it means to be mature. But mature is precisely what undergraduates cannot be expected to be. And while the help that an academic institution can give will not—and should not try to—prevent all mistakes, it can substantially improve the choices students make. Approaches that vary from repeated conversations with a knowledgeable and sympathetic person to the taking of batteries of tests can materially assist in converting those educational offerings into genuine opportunities.

A good deal of knowledge is thus needed if one is to make good educational choices, if the institutions' clients are to give their informed consent. But most students will need an additional sort of paraeducation at the beginning of their academic careers, if they are to be effective learners in the new environment to which they have come. Part of that paraeducation might be called practical. As newcomers to a complex institution, these students are strangers who need a map, intelligible to them, of the bureaucratic paths by means of which possibilities are made actual, especially in larger universities. How often do students realize too late what they might have been able to do had they known how at an earlier time! Creators of bureaucratic hurdles are obligated to teach those confronted with them how to overcome them. Still another part of that map must show the institutional resources—from libraries to counseling services—that are available to clients, and there must be instruction on how they are effectively used.

A different kind of preparatory mission must introduce students to what might be called the *way* of higher education. If only by virtue of the pluralist character of education in America, students come to college with a large range of abilities and training in broadly applicable skills and attitudes important for development and cultivation throughout the undergraduate years. Newcomers will vary in their abilities to read reflectively, think analytically, engage in discussion that combines openness to the views of others with a recognition that the merit of all views is dependent on supporting evidence. It cannot even be taken for granted that secondary schools have acquainted all of their students with the style of intellectual discourse that allows for inconclusiveness as an outcome of inquiry and debate, leaving questions without answers and disagreements without resolution. Accordingly, if they are to thrive in their new intellectual environment, a signal must be given to the newly arrived, and not merely a symbolic one, to the effect that most of them will encounter a significant break between the ways of the educational phase recently concluded and those of the educational venture now beginning.

All colleges admit adolescents, that is to say, persons not yet mature; all colleges admit persons who are antecedently unacquainted with the complex ins and outs of the institution to which they are admitted; most institutions admit students inadequately prepared to participate fully in the educational process, or at least in some segments of it. For the most part—at least with respect to undergraduate study—the admitting academic institutions take these steps knowingly; that is, they invite persons to become their students, about whom they have reason to believe that they are deficient in various ways to take satisfactory advantage of the opportunities that will there be offered to them. Of course, the enrolling students have an obligation to strive to overcome such inadequacies, even to a greater degree than that to which all students must participate in their own education by working hard. However, the admitting institution has an obligation, as well, to assist with the bridging of these various gaps. Whatever the magnitude of the effort different students might make, however varied their successes and failures, the institution has a duty to do what it can to enable its students to do their best.

The term "paraeducation" has been used to refer to a variety of functions, the carrying out of which I regard as obligatory for IHEs, especially but not only for those with undergraduate programs. That somewhat ugly term may be unfamiliar, but the activities that are subsumed under it most certainly are not. But the full meaning of conventional terms that refer to those activites—"advising," "counseling," "orientation"—is no longer grasped by those who use them, a fact that makes it particularly difficult to persuade people that they have a moral obligation to see to it that they are satisfactorily carried out. All too often, in the academy, the deterioration of the functions so designated parallels the degeneration of "informed consent" in the medical world. "Advising" as bored enunciation of bureaucratic rules; "counseling" as the dispensing of canned advice; "orientation" by way of handing out sheaves of paper detailing information about the library and recreational athletic facilities. What students need is indeed *advice*, and *counsel*, and to be *oriented* to the ways of the institution, but in ways that pertain to them as individuals, in ways that help them convert opportunities into actualities for them. *That* is what IHEs are obligated to do.

Notes

1. MSA, 1994, 1.
2. NEAS&C, 1992, 1.
3. MSA, 1994, 1.
4. AAUP, 1995, 106; also see, below, Appendix 2, 131.
5. "Statement of the Association's Council: Freedom and Responsibility," 107–8; "Joint Statement on Rights and Freedom of Students," 227–233, AAUP, 1995.
6. AHA, 1995, 3.
7. APSA, 1991, 10.
8. MLA, 1992, 7; also see, below, Appendix 3, 135.
9. APSA, 1991, 10–12.
10. AALS, 1996, 2; also see, below, Appendix 4, 143.
11. ASA, 1997, 16; italics added.
12. See, for example, Bayles, 1989, 85, 103–4, chapter 8.
13. AAUP, 1995, 105; also see, below, Appendix 2, 131.
14. To date, these are the products of the American Association for Higher Education's (AAHE) Teaching Initiative: Edgerton, 1991; Hutchings, 1995; Hutchings, 1996; Hutchings, 1997. Excerpts are reprinted, below, as Appendix 5 (A), (B), and (C).
15. E.g., Hutchings, 1996, chapter 2; also see, below, Appendix 5 (B).

16. E.g., Hutchings, 1996, chapter 5, and Edgerton, 1991; also see, below, Appendix 5 (A).

17. E.g., Hutchings, 1996, chapter 9.

18. Hutchings, 1996, chapters 1, 3, 4, 6, 7, and 8, respectively. For a pioneering study see Katz and Henry, 1988.

19. See chapter 9, "Support," in Weingartner, 1993, 139–154.

20. See chapter 2, sections I and II.

21. The discussion to follow leans heavily on the section "Paraeducational Goals" in Weingartner, 1993, 113–118. It includes quotations from that discussion, without quotation marks, near-quotations, and paraphrases. With permission from Oryx Press, the publisher.

Chapter 5

Quality: Research

I. Policies

"Because researchers are professionals who have received training, education, and benefits from society, they have the traditional trustee's responsibility to preserve, develop, and extend the intellectual assets that they have received (in part) from the public and that they hold in trust for that society."[1] This quotation is very much in the spirit of what has been maintained all along. Academics are in effect trained as researchers; thus, in contrast to their roles as teachers, no paradox is generated when it is asserted that academics should practice their professions. Everything should also be quite straightforward for our topic of academic administration: The obligation just expressed for faculty members translates into the obligation for academic administrators to create the conditions that make it possible for faculty members to engage in scholarship

Of course what those conditions actually amount to varies much with fields of inquiry. Perhaps the only component they all have in common is that most precious of commodities: time. Institutionally, this can mean the assignment of teaching duties that allow time for research activities or of the award of periodic research leaves, or both. Other needed resources vary immensely—from space, to library holdings, to equipment of every kind and staff support that make library holdings and equipment usable.

But to point just to the physical support required for all the scholarly activities by members of the academy quickly stops us in our tracks. For we surely delude ourselves if we suppose that even the richest and most comprehensive of research universities could come anywhere close to providing what it takes for all faculty members in whatever field to work on the scholarly projects their abilities and energy can generate. IHEs are not research institutes (even if some units within them occa-

65

sionally resemble these), so that it is an exception when a college or university can provide everything researchers need—a rare exception in the natural sciences, less rare in the humanities and the social sciences. Thus, assuming wise deployment of resources—a matter surely not to be taken for granted—just what is the obligation of administrators?

Their most obvious task is to devise and administer policies that facilitate faculty members' access to resources. One might well think that this point is so obvious as not to require spelling out. For is the situation not analogous to that of the corporate executive who surely does not need to be told to provide the machinery his employees require if they are to be productive? Perhaps the reference to "employees" tips us off to some differences, since it is a term not beloved by faculty members. Indeed, at many a university, faculty members resemble independent contractors more than they do functionaries of the institution, if only because in their scholarship they largely address peers outside their own institutions; they work to please distant specialists rather than local authorities. Perhaps in part because of this faculty detachment from the sheltering institution, the primary goal of a research administration most often is not the facilitating of research, but protecting the institution from possible transgressions by its researchers. Of course, laws and regulations necessitate some defensive administration, and prudence calls for it, both with respect to research integrity and to the management of federal and other outside funds. But it remains true that it is also prudent for an institution (manufacturing or educational) to do what it takes for its "workers" to get the job done they are hired to do. And unless such people are also selected for the ability to negotiate obstacle courses, it is also right for the institution to facilitate the performance of tasks that are then evaluated, with rewards dependent on the assessments made.

If the exhortation to support faculty research applies without hesitation to research universities, the picture becomes much more complicated when one looks at the *entire* collectivity of American IHEs—39 percent of which, remember, are two-year institutions; many others are small, poorly endowed, four-year colleges. Those 3,706 establishments, then, vary immensely and perhaps in nothing as much as in the research components of their missions. Only a fraction—and not a large one— have the capacity to support research seriously in a significant range of academic fields and provide the needed physical underpinnings and limited teaching duties. Many institutions do not support faculty scholarship at all—a far larger number than appears to be assumed by those who write about the world of higher education, perhaps because they themselves tend to be housed in institutions that prize research.

Two sets of conclusions for academic administrators can be drawn from this broader picture. Above all, administrators have the obligation to ensure that institutional practices are consistent with each other. Specifically, three sets of policies must cohere: those pertaining to the hiring of faculty members, those regarding the support of research activities, and those governing the ways in which faculty members are rewarded for their services. It is not difficult to envisage how faculty members would be mistreated where these policies fail to conform to each other. Faculty members might be appointed, for example, wrongly believing that the research they are trained to do and interested in pursuing is supported by the institution. On the other side, without being aware of it at the time of hiring, faculty members may discover that they are expected to engage in scholarship they are not interested in or even qualified for. Perhaps more commonly, the powers that determine salaries or promotions make evaluations on bases different from those apparent to candidates at the time of hiring, or the committees and administrators that recommend and act on salaries and promotions expect research accomplishments, the achieving of which is not supported by the institution. In all such instances of policy incoherence, faculty members are caught in some middle and stand to suffer treatment from their institution that is unfair or worse.

Faculty members, however, would not be the only casualties of such incoherence of policies. Unfairness rankles and affects behavior, as does frustrated ambition. Put bluntly, faculty who feel themselves mistreated are unlikely to do their best; they will tend to devote time and energy, furthermore, to politicking aimed at rectifying their situation. One result is certain: the institution also suffers and is likely to fall short of doing as well as it might, with students the probable victims.

Such situations are among the consequences of unclarity about an institution's mission or of disagreements about it, tacit or explicit. The importance of agreement and clarity about what a college or university seeks to accomplish and the need for that to be understood by all of its members, faculty as well as administrators, are heightened by the fact that the policies in question may well be formulated in different parts of the academic forest and implemented by different groups of people. There is no invisible hand that will work for coherence. On the contrary, as noted before, the interests and forces that propel these departments and committees are most often centrifugal, making incoherence the natural condition and coherence the product of labor, self-consciously undertaken.[3] What is needed is a sheet of music from which everyone can sing and an academic administration that conducts its unruly chorus in such a way that everyone actually does sing from that sheet.

A second set of issues pertains to the complex relationship between research and teaching. To begin with, it is well recognized that faculty members' research activities can interfere with their teaching obligations and often do. Although teaching assignments at research universities are usually limited so as to leave time for scholarship, the pressure to be productive is also the most intense in just those institutions. Administrators can certainly help by supporting this function in ways that have already been discussed. But equally important is the manner in which a faculty member's scholarship is evaluated and rewarded; for however much the standing of researchers depends on the views of fellow investigators in the field, faculty members' employing institutions are not without influence on their behavior. To this topic we shall turn shortly, after considering the institution for which research by faculty members is not a major desideratum or one at all.

We will here assume that there is no problem with regard to the coherence of institutional policies vis-à-vis faculty members in such institutions, though that cannot be taken for granted. It will not do to impose massive teaching loads on faculty members, provide them with little or no support for scholarly activities, and then nevertheless use achievement in research as a significant determinant when they are reviewed for salary increases or promotions. But beyond this point about fairness in the treatment of faculty members, some further considerations must be put forward concerning IHEs that care little or nothing about faculty research and fail to support it.

II. The Necessity of Research

One might say that yet another paradox is created when at an IHE no opportunity is given for faculty members to engage in research, not to mention having such an establishment actually frown on and discourage scholarship. At such a place, not only are faculty members hired to perform tasks—namely teach—that they were not trained for, but they are prevented from doing that which their professional education has prepared them to do. A doctoral education is not like the filling of some giant bucket, so that, once filled, bits from its contents can be distributed during a lifetime of teaching. Rather, that education merely transfers a limited quantity of material into the bucket and puts much effort into teaching graduate students to use a shovel, so as to enable them to augment and renew that content during an entire career. Indeed, students are likely to have chosen to undertake so lengthy and demanding a course precisely because they wanted to spend their lives in the exploration of such scholarly areas as history or physics or French literature or whatever.

Nevertheless, it is not unreasonable to take a tough line concerning this paradox of research, especially during an era in which the activities of the market have come to be regarded as the most beneficial regulator of all areas of life. "People make mistakes regarding the careers they propose to pursue," goes the argument. "It's too bad when they select a course that becomes obsolete before their careers can begin to flourish, and so it is ill-fated when they select a metier in which eligible applicants vastly outnumber available opportunities. Similarly, it is unfortunate when grasp exceeds reach, as it does when people embark on careers without sufficient talent to enable them to thrive. Even in lean years positions become available in research universities, though of course far fewer than there are aspirants. Those who are not among the very best may then have to make do with careers that fall far short of their expectations. Aspiring academics are no different from youngsters who attend law school expecting to plead constitutional cases before the Supreme Court, but spend their lives, instead, closing real estate transactions and writing the wills of their neighbors. Life can be tough; but perhaps, as in Candide's world, the market, even when so wasteful, is the best possible mechanism precisely because the other possible ones are even worse."

Consider such a declaration to be a reluctant acceptance of the wisdom of the day regarding the relationship between the expectations of potential faculty members and the obligations toward them of hiring institutions. But if the fact that faculty members have certain desires or aspirations does not obligate their institutions to be responsive to them, there is more to be said about the question as to whether IHEs have obligations to foster faculty research. So far, we have regarded scholarship as an activity that aims to achieve advances in different fields of inquiry. The *results* research activities bring about have been in focus, with research universities thought of as places where people make contributions to knowledge. But in the pluralist system of American postsecondary education, other types of academic institutions are to be found. And quite a few of these might well declare, with emphasis, "We are not in the business of advancing the frontiers of knowledge; that job we leave to the bigger boys who can afford to do so; our mission is confined to teaching; that and only that is what we pay our faculty to do." The reputations of such institutions thus do not hang from discoveries made by their faculties or from the books and articles they publish. Their merit is dependent, instead, on the quality of the teaching programs in the areas in which they function.

But to accept such a division of labor in the world of higher education does not close the discussion of research by faculty members. For in addition to considering the effects of research on the growth of knowledge, we must also look at how engaging in the activity is related to teaching. For many, a conventional view that claims being an active scholar is necessary for adequate teaching at the level of higher education is simply not credible, at least not for a significant portion of the curriculum. Yes, it makes sense to require those who teach graduate students to work at the frontiers of their fields. But that insistence seems to have as little relevance for teaching introductory and other bread-and-butter undergraduate courses as it does for teaching history or chemistry in high school. While there is a need to keep up-to-date in the teacher's field—more in some than in others—that is most effectively achieved with refresher courses or summer seminars, just as is encouraged or required of teachers in many secondary schools.

For a substantial part of the curriculum of a "teaching institution," in other words, instructors need not work to extend the frontiers of knowledge or even be familiar with them, since the courses they teach remain well within the center of that realm. Faculty research, therefore, is irrelevant in such institutions, so that supporting it expends resources that might be better used to reduce the size of classes or to improve the equipment students use in their laboratory sessions. And to the extent to which such teaching institutions must offer a limited number of genuinely advanced courses, let them deploy a modest number of specialists to teach them and make ad hoc arrangements to support a certain amount of research or, more simply, underwrite periodic refresher courses.

All this may sound plausible, but it is not without its problems. In their impact on postsecondary teaching, are refresher courses an adequate substitute for engaging in research? What is the effect on an institution of having its faculty consist of a smaller group of specialists who are teaching scholars and a larger hoi polloi who teach the bulk of the curriculum? *Higher* education, one must insist, is not just *more* education, but is in at least one respect distinctively different from most, if not all of, earlier education. For teaching at that level, even in beginning courses, must include the introduction of students to a field of *inquiry* and not be limited simply to acquainting them with a distillate of results-I-know-not-how-attained. An important goal of all higher education is to assure that students become inquirers, even where they do not become (or desire to become) specialists in a field. If so, teaching, in higher education—and not just in advanced courses—does not consist only of imparting information and developing the intellectual techniques pertaining to the fields taught, but of fostering the habits, attitudes, and abilities of someone who is an inquirer, able to recognize and formulate problems and to devise methods to solve them.*

I will here make no attempt to further characterize this important goal, except to note that this formulation must not mislead one into thinking of it as a *single* goal.[2] While it makes sense to say of someone that he or she possesses an inquiring mind, this phrase merely denotes a desire to know and a willingness to try to find out. However, the ability to go from such a potentiality to actual inquiry is not singular, but varies from one field of inquiry to the next. There can thus be no course, Introduction to Inquiry, for that introduction must be embedded in most every course and will differ markedly as one goes from chemistry, to history, to literature, to engineering, to anthropology, and so on. The consequences for our topic are obvious. *Those who are to foster in students the habits, attitudes, and abilities of an inquirer must themselves possess those traits.* Moreover, these attributes are not retained, once acquired, whether or not they are used. They are not so much like the ability to swim, preserved even after years of disuse, but they resemble the pliancy of muscles that is maintained only if the muscles are employed. In sum, for students to be taught in ways appropriate to higher education, their teachers must be actively engaged in scholarship.

All teachers in *all* courses? An affirmative answer would imply too simplistic a view of IHEs. There is room in places as complex as colleges and universities for such roles as lecturers in language, teachers of composition, instructors in certain basic mathematics courses, all of them exempted from the requirement—and the opportunity!—to be active as scholars in their fields. However, the number of part-time and other nonregular (nontenure track) faculty must be limited; this cadre should constitute a considerably smaller portion of the total faculty than is now so often the case.

More than one reason supports this recommendation, but an obvious, though important, one arises in the present context. For when one looks at the composition of an IHE as a whole, one faces the potentiality of having quantitative changes become an undesirable change in quality.

---

*In actuality, the distinction between higher education and the education that precedes it is of course not as sharp as is here formulated. Many a teacher in secondary school manages to nurture inquiring minds, while students trying to learn French are better off with such virtues as diligence than with the spirit of inquiry. But, first, the fact that some of the goals of higher education are already fostered in secondary education does not diminish their importance in the post-secondary realm. And, second, beginning language or basic mathematics are not typical undergraduate courses and might not be offered for college credit at all if they were taught more commonly and more effectively in high school and if there were not so close a link between credits needed for graduation and tuition fees.

Two sets of characteristics are required if there is to be an IHE. On the one hand, there must be what might be called an appropriate "form": a suitable organization, a fitting set of policies, procedures, and goals. On the other, there is the matter of an institution's "content": the people who inhabit it and engage in its activities. These, too, must be appropriate to the task in that they possess the traits of academics—a certain range of abilities, habits, and desires. To be sure, it has been avowed that IHEs are complex, and given the responsibilities assigned to their faculties, there is room—indeed, need—for more than one kind of person. However, as the mix changes from mostly teacher-scholars to a large minority or more of part-time and adjunct faculty whose teaching is not informed by their own activities as inquirers, so do the tone and ethos of the institution. To this transformation of the institution as a whole we must add the fact that typical distributions of teaching loads bring undergraduates disproportionately into more frequent contact with such nonregular faculty members—sometimes at high tuition costs. For those undergraduates, then, the deterioration of their place of study from that of a genuine IHE is amplified. For once again we see that the proposal to deploy, in an institution primarily devoted to teaching, a limited number of specialists engaged in research, while leaving the bulk of the teaching to those who are only so occupied, is not an acceptable one.*

III. Evaluation

In spite of the contention earlier put forward—and with emphasis—that a major obligation of academic administrators is to foster, in every way, the teaching functions of the faculty, it has just now been argued that they have a duty to foster research as well. Unfortunately, the best way of reconciling these competing demands is utopian: to have a budget so huge that it can, among other things, support a faculty large enough to enable the institution to get its teaching done well and conscientiously, while the teaching duties for each faculty member leave him or her adequate time for scholarly work. But, alas, we cannot maintain that institu-

---

*As the trend continues that reduces the proportion of faculty members hired to be full-time teacher/scholars, a still larger issue is broached. As students consider the careers to which they might wish to devote their lives, they are being confronted by a changing academic world. It is not unreasonable to suppose that some of the most able and creative will decide to pursue other professions when they see that the proportion of positions for postsecondary teachers who are also supported in research is decreasing. Current institutional practices, in other words, may well contribute to a future decline in the quality and vitality of the world of higher education.

tions and their administrators are obligated to have enormous budgets. All we can ask of them is that they spend their money wisely and thus give the highest priority to these two central functions of any IHE. But other things can be done as well, though nothing will wholly eliminate the competition between teaching and research.

Academic administrators, recall, have a leading role—often a determinative role—in the evaluation of faculty members and in setting rewards based on those evaluations. This being so, we will be well served by some reflection on these evaluations. As already noted in the discussion of teaching, conventional wisdom in the academy sees a notable difference between the evaluation of the teaching of faculty members and the evaluation of their research. The former has been thought to be so fraught with subjectivity that it had best not serve as a basis for actions that seriously affect the lives of faculty members. On the other side, it is usually held to be perfectly possible to do a decent job of evaluating faculty research, provided proper procedures are employed. But this difference begins to shrink once the evaluation of teaching is taken seriously, for then, it turns out, numerous methods can be devised that will credibly accomplish that task, singly or in combination. The contrast pales further if one does not simply accept hallowed beliefs about the evaluation of research, but raises questions about that process instead.

The comfort with accepted ways of assessing faculty research is rooted in the fact that the job is thought of as being turned over to the disciplines to which the work belongs. And it is surely right—and the professional thing to do—that historians sit in judgment on the work of historians, physicists evaluate contributions to physics, and so on. Yet the process seems so cut-and-dried, in good part just because that is how those who participate in it often treat it. Acknowledged or not, there is collaboration between the discipline and the institution of the faculty member whose work is under scrutiny. The process quickly becomes less routine when attention is paid to the questions the institution asks of the disciplines.*

Such a discussion is best opened with a recantation of the oversimple view of research and scholarship so far adopted in this chapter.** We

---

*Moreover, when one thinks of the higher education establishment as a whole, it is worth noting that for most disciplines, just about all members are also members of specific academic institutions. And, given that these institutions are also the sources of their livelihoods, it is unduly modest to suppose that the institutions are wholly without influence.

**What follows is intended as an epistemology-free epistemology of a sampling of the variety of products that are looked at under the heading of faculty research, without meaning to presuppose some particular philosophical position about the nature of knowledge.

have spoken of "contributions to knowledge" and of "pushing outward the frontiers of knowledge," though there is much to be evaluated that is not covered by such phrases. Most obviously, it is not to knowledge that artist/faculty of every variety contribute. The work of painters, composers, poets, novelists, filmmakers, lighting directors, not to mention performers of all kinds, is judged by many different criteria, none of which is a measure of their contributions to knowledge. Nor is this phrase appropriate for many whose home in the academy goes back to the first founding of universities. For it is at best dubious to call a new interpretation of Plato's *Republic* a contribution to knowledge or a fresh reading of Genesis or of *Measure for Measure* or even a reinterpretation of Trotsky's role in the Russian Revolution. In such cases, the writers put forward opinions, which others find interesting or boring, stimulating or obfuscating, fresh or stale, etc. And while readers will look for arguments that bolster those opinions and for evidence that supports them, they may never get around to asking the question, "Is what this writer is saying true?" Even in the most traditional scholarship in the humanities and history—taking the form of editions, biographies, archival investigations—readers pay much less attention to new nuggets that might have been tossed into the bucket of knowledge than to the insight that is (or is not) provided by the piece of work under consideration. Unless a researcher gets the facts wrong or makes some startling new discovery, that is what reviewers both in learned and more popular journals are likely to attend to.

The sciences, including the "hardest," resemble this picture much more than might meet the eye. A paper in a science—natural or social— may depict another way of looking at something; it may propose new techniques for analyzing certain data; it may point up connections hitherto not seen or not adequately attended to; it may criticize some chunk of accepted theory or propose an alternative to such a piece of received wisdom. All this and more, besides those reports of "findings" as a result of experiments or surveys or clinical trials that permit us to say unambiguously that now we know something we didn't know before. And if, conventionally, mathematics is the "hardest" science of them all, one has to be a rabid Platonist to claim that researchers at that domain's many frontiers discover truths, rather than devise, contrive, invent.

The picture becomes yet more variegated if we branch out from this quick once-over of the arts and sciences to research that is undertaken in professional schools—from law to engineering, from medicine to library science, from special education to marketing. Not only does one confront deep dissimilarities as one goes from one such area to another, but within each, research products can differ markedly from each other, as one moves along the continuum from theoretical to applied, with the contrivance of that better mousetrap as the model at one end.

This recitation could be much expanded, but enough has been said to support two lines of thought. Note, first, that the so prevalent view of how research is to be evaluated rests on the *decision* to keep the process simple, not on a *fact* about the complexity of the material to be evaluated. The decision is, in effect, to draw one's conclusions as much as possible from information that is either quantifiable or has other hallmarks of objectivity. To rest a case on the number of publications is ideal. The number is a quantity; there are more or fewer of them; and a publication is a piece of work that has been given a stamp of approval by an acceptance process that is held to be impartial. And given that there are lots of periodicals and presses that do the publishing, each field generates a pecking order, going from most prestigious to least, about which there is the kind of broad agreement that confers a stamp of near-objectivity. In addition, letters of recommendation are solicited from colleagues in the discipline that ask about the candidate's standing in such a way so as to yield responses that tend to be based on essentially the same information, held to be objective. One might conclude, only exaggerating somewhat, that what is looked at is not so much a faculty member's research, but the package in which that work is wrapped.

Such a procedure contrasts sharply with the assessment of the *quality* of research, with attention paid only secondarily to quantity. The evaluators' concerns center on how important a piece of work is, how it might influence others, how interesting it is, whether respondents from the discipline recommend their students attend to this work, and the like. In short, while academic institutions must continue to go to the disciplines for much of the evaluation of their faculty's research, they are in a position to change the manner in which that assessment is made by the questions that are put to the spokespersons for the disciplines.

But why bother to urge these changes? There are two major reasons, both of them pertaining to the obligations of academic administrators. First, probably the single most important contribution an academic administration can make to reducing the tension between faculty members' roles as teachers and as researchers—and to free them, so to speak, to devote more time and energy to teaching—is to move from basing personnel judgments on research quantity to making the work's quality primary. No one doubts that the hectic life of faculty members, especially junior faculty, is rooted in the fact that research quantity is so central to their future. The rat race is to do enough to satisfy the powers that be, and since it is never so clear just how much it takes, the safe thing is to do more.* We know that doing more research takes more time; the relationship between time and better, more significant research is not so obvious. Moreover, by liberating the evaluators from counting publications—that is, completed projects—it also frees them to consider work in progress, enabling them to assess both the quality of the work being done and the progress that is made between appraisals. As a consequence of shifting from quantity to quality as the prime criterion, another way is opened up for reducing the time pressure imposed upon faculty members, enabling them to give greater attention to teaching.

However, a policy that pays serious attention to work that has not yet been completed would also contribute importantly to the second goal that a shift in criteria from quantity to quality would bring about. Complaints are ubiquitous about the vastness of the number of scholarly publications that the American professoriate produces and about the triviality, indeed, senselessness, of so much of it.** Nor must this excess be regarded only as the production of something that no one needs. The expense of creating, disseminating, and housing this output is immense, not to mention what it costs scholars to sort through these mountains of paper in their attempts to keep up with their fields. The waste is great and, among other things, contributes significantly to the high and ever-increasing cost of higher education. But the primary engines that propel this monster in overdrive are the processes by which faculty members are everywhere evaluated for the determination of actions that affect their careers and livelihood. And the drivers of these engines are, above all, academic administrators. Were they to be more discriminate, in the sense here suggested, faculty/researchers would be more discriminate in the research projects they select and carry out. On the one hand, more large—and, one hopes, more significant—projects could be undertaken, since the postponement of publication would not automatically be detri-

---

*Interestingly—amusingly?—in a 1982 report by the Association of American Medical Colleges on the maintenance of high ethical standards in research, only two recommendations aim at prevention (while many others are concerned with policing). One of these is "that the quality rather than quantity of research [be] emphasized as a criterion for the promotion of faculty," presumably as a way of removing motives to take unethical shortcuts (reported in Steneck, 1984, 7).

**These issues are hardly new. A long time ago, Leibniz wrote, in his *Memoir for Enlightened Persons of Good Intention*: "And for those intellectuals capable of contributing to the increase of knowledge, they should think of projects which not only serve to get them known and applauded but also to produce new knowledge . . . for to write for writing's sake is only a bad habit, and to write merely to make people talk about us is a wicked vanity, which even does harm to others by making them lose their time in useless reading" (quoted in Baier, 1980, 82–83).

mental to a career. On the other hand, the total research output would be smaller and its quality higher. Add to these socially useful effects the fact that the competition between teaching and research, though surely not eliminated, would be reduced, and the obligations of administrators would seem to be obvious.

IV. Pedagogical Research

The second benefit to be derived from beginning a discussion of research with a realistic look at the range of activities and products that are to be found under this heading is that such a look should discourage counterproductive purism. Purism, says my dictionary, is "rigid adherence to, or insistence upon, purity." That attitude dismisses all kinds of enterprises as "not really research" and is the attitude of academic administrators at least as often as it is of representatives of the disciplines. And for two reasons counterproductive, because often what is thus dismissed has value (in the straightforward sense of being useful) and because no one other than "misguided" faculty members either could or would undertake these tasks. While different kinds of applied research might be cited as examples, I want particularly to single out what I shall call pedagogical research.

With this phrase I mean to refer to many different kinds of investigations that aim at discovering how instructors, alone or with various types of aid from their institutions, can improve the learning of students. I say "pedagogical research" to distinguish my proposal from Ernest Boyer's "scholarship of teaching."[5] If I read him correctly, he maintains that much (or all?) teaching simply *is* scholarship, because whoever teaches might (does?) learn by teaching. However, even if it were inevitable that teachers learn through teaching—which, alas, it surely is not—it is hard to see what is gained by this identification. Those to whom it matters that faculty members engage in scholarship, including this writer, will not give up the requirement that scholarly activity aims at creating a product that is subject to scrutiny by professional peers. Those colleagues are then in a position to benefit from the work done, to build on it in their own work, as well as to criticize it and point out its inadequacies. For reasons that do not need spelling out, students are not such peers, so that whatever else might be claimed for teaching, it is not, in an important sense, scholarship.*

---

*But note that many of the tables in Boyer's book, reporting on an extensive "National Survey of Faculty, 1989" by the Carnegie Foundation for the Advancement of Teaching, show that a significant fraction of the country's faculty is critical of the manner in which they are evaluated. For example, 68 percent

Some pedagogical scholarship will not be subject matter specific and is likely to be the work of professional educators in the sense of professors of education or of psychologists who are concerned with learning. Such enterprises, however, do not need special mention here, since they are perfectly analogous to historians writing historical monographs or lawyers writing articles in law reviews. The part of pedagogical research I particularly want to draw attention to is likely to be specific to a certain subject matter (history), perhaps quite narrowly conceived (the French Revolution), and may, less frequently, be specific to certain subclasses of students as well (teaching English to immigrants from Vietnam). Such research may well start out as experimentation, by teachers, with ways of conveying material to their students and lead, when successful, to the discovery of ways in which instructors—with or without different kinds of aid from the institution—become more effective in assisting their students to learn. Improved pedagogy, however, becomes pedagogical scholarship only when it takes a form that makes it accessible to others, whether as a publication or-conference report. Only then can the pedagogical researcher's work be used by others and tested; then to be supported, or criticized, or built upon. Such research products, moreover, can differ much in elaborateness: be more or less complex; apply to a broader or narrower span of subject matter; include more or less evidence supporting the pedagogical claims put forward; and so on. In short, pedagogical research resembles subject matter scholarship in important ways and can take the form that enables evaluators to make judgments with respect to its magnitude, usefulness, and, in various ways, quality.

So there is a sense in which pedagogical research does not push outward the frontiers of knowledge; but it does fulfill two important functions stressed earlier. First, such investigations can well serve the purpose of helping the investigator retain the kind of inquiring mind that is so necessary for the teachers of students acquiring a postsecondary education. To be sure, we need the proviso "other things being equal," but that kind of reservation also holds for substantive research. Just as much of that mountain of inconsequential research earlier referred to— most of it in conventionally accepted fields—may indeed be the product of activity that is essentially mindless, so may pedagogical research be routine, mechanical, and do nothing for the investigator's brain. But meritorious pedagogical research requires a similar kind of self-consciousness about the subject matter being taught, as does creditable sub-

of all respondents agree that "At My Institution We Need Better Ways, Besides Publications, to Evaluate the Scholarly Performance of the Faculty" (Boyer, 1990, 34).

stantive scholarship, and thus similarly contributes to the maintenance of the quality of mind appropriate to faculty members of IHEs.

Second, the point of pedagogical research is to contribute to improved teaching, to make students more effective learners. By its very conception, this is research that promotes teaching. To the degree to which members of an IHE are fruitfully engaged in pedagogical research, to that degree the teaching at that institution is improved and a central institutional function is better fulfilled. To be sure, because of their competing claims on time and energy, the tension between teaching and scholarship does not disappear even for someone engaged in pedagogical research. However, it is precisely this kind of research that is most appropriately encouraged and supported in institutions that think of themselves primarily as teaching institutions, since it will help to make them better at carrying out their missions.

A final point, made from the perspective of the higher education establishment as a whole. It was pointed out earlier that only in relatively recent years has it been generally acknowledged that effective teaching cannot be taken for granted from everyone who has mastered the subject matter to be taught, that there are things to be investigated and learned about teaching, at the undergraduate level and beyond. Now, it is surely the case that individual instructors can improve their own teaching by learning from those who make it their profession to study learning processes, or from those who think about the institutionalization of effective teaching, and so on. But such broad approaches will take practitioners in the classroom only so far. While there may be many general truths about effective teaching, there will be many more that are specific to different subject matter. "Wholesale" strategies must be supplemented by "retail" ones, by methods that pertain to this particular domain, while being largely or wholly irrelevant to others. And only those who have specific substantive knowledge can do that retail work; only they are in a position to contribute to the improvement of teaching in those subjects. Accordingly, if teaching is to be improved in diverse subject areas, IHEs must foster pedagogical research on the part of their faculties.

Teaching and research are the central objectives of IHEs, even for the multiversity with a complex mission that resembles a major shopping mall. With respect to both, there is much to do for academic administrators, even though they themselves carry out neither of these functions. Indeed, there are many things they ought to do as the agents of institutions that by their very nature incur obligations. In this and the preceding chapter, I have given an account of some of the more important roles they must play in these two domains. After a brief coda, I turn to some of the issues that arise when one looks at academic administrators as supervisors of numerous processes ongoing in IHEs.

V. A Coda on Trying Harder

To Immanuel Kant, a very stern moralist, is also attributed the comforting thought that *ought implies can*.[6] Comforting, because this dictum entails that we do not have a duty to do what we cannot do. Even though a child has fallen off the bridge into the river, if I cannot swim, I am not obligated to leap after him so as to try to bring him to shore. While this maxim applies to academic administrators as it does to the rest of humankind, it does not license a lazy jump to the excusing conclusion that "I can't do *that!*" Indeed, in the realm of activities administrators engage in, it is often not possible to determine whether some goal can or cannot be achieved, except by making serious efforts to accomplish it. One's knowledge of how a particular group of people will behave under envisaged new circumstances (which is what is involved in predicting whether some administrative move will accomplish the sought-after goal) is often so flimsy that where the goal is sufficiently important to warrant incurring some risks, it is appropriate to stick closer to the spirit of Kant and test whether one can accomplish one's aim by trying.

But there is more to it than acting in the spirit of Kant. For with respect to many activities central to the role of academic administrators, there is a duty to try hard, for there certainly are occasions where it is also true that *can implies ought*. Clearly it would be absurd to elevate that italicized phrase to the status of universal principle. There is lots we can do that we are not at all obligated to do; indeed, there is no shortage of examples where we are able to act in some way, but, emphatically, have the duty to refrain from doing so. But the context of a professional institution makes all the difference. If it can save the life of an injured person, a hospital is obligated to do its best to do so—a duty owed to the medical profession, as well as to the patient. Similarly, academic institutions owe it to their profession to provide as good an education for their students as they are able, and they owe that to those students who have entrusted their educations to them. The fact that mitigating or excusing circumstances can account for exceptions does not undermine the general rule. Stores that sell shoddy merchandise and give poor service may be imprudent to risk being put out of business by a paucity of customers. Academic institutions that *cannot* perform competently or *will* not do their best are doing wrong: the quality of their achievements has moral dimensions.

Academic administrators, as important contributors to the education of an IHE's students, are thus not only the assignees of numerous obligations owed by the institution they serve, but also the duty to do the best they can. But what does it mean for them to try hard? As a group, they are an overworked lot, daily chasing from meeting to meeting and staying late to catch up on correspondence and piles of paperwork. What more can they be asked to do than to keep up with these unceasing demands? The answer is: some sorting out; prioritizing, to use an ugly word.

A good deal of the frenzied administrative activity is doubtlessly unavoidable. Much decision making in the academy is collaborative; this makes many a time-consuming meeting necessary. Myriad tasks are mandated by laws or by governing boards. Many of these bureaucratic requirements are not necessarily wise—that myriad is a plethora—but discharging them is a condition of the job. All the same, the purpose of many a meeting is not collaboration, but a way of avoiding taking responsibility. Numerous, unneeded bureaucratic chores are self-imposed or inflicted by one academic administrator on another, many of them based on the widespread but dubious assumption that the multiplication of such moves prevents mistakes or at least deflects blame. Finally, poor deployment of administrative personnel or an inability to delegate can contribute to that surfeit of meetings and chores.

But to the degree to which this proliferation of unneeded tasks takes away from the zeal with which central institutional excellences are pursued, it is wrong, because these pursuits stand in service to the institution's clients, from its current students to society at large. The realization that this is so does not, of course, require administrators to be insubordinate and act in ways that would be tantamount to professional suicide. Nor is an administrator obligated to assume the mantle of reformer and try to reverse pervasive tendencies of our age. For, at best, the undertaking of such a mission is supererogatory, beyond the call of duty; more likely, it is quixotic and counterproductive. However, in view of the existence of powerful primary obligations to shape an excellent IHE, it becomes a duty for an administrator to sort out which busy-making demands (demands preventing the pursuit of central goals) are of the comfort-making sort, as opposed to those that are truly unavoidable. The former ought then be abolished, and organizational moves should be considered to reduce the hampering effect of the latter. Academic administration is not a job, but a calling.

Notes

1. Shrader-Frechette, 1994, 24.
2. For a more extensive discussion of related issues, see Weingartner, 1993, chapter 6.

3. See chapter 3, section II, and Weingartner, 1996, xiii and *passim*.

4. Steneck, 1984, 7.

5. Boyer, 1990, 23–25.

6. Attributed to Kant, but never so formulated by him; indeed, he is by no means aiming to relieve us of any duties where he makes the connection between *ought* and *can*. See Kant, 1956, 30 and 163, and Kant, 1991, 186. I am grateful to Professor Stephen Engstrom for these references.

Chapter 6

Supervision

I. Managing People

The main topic of this chapter is the consideration of some of the moral implications of supervisory activities on the parts of academic administrators vis-à-vis the faculty of an IHE. That, after all, is the administrative business peculiar to the academic world. In the academy, however, a good deal of "ordinary" administration is also to be found: in the relationship of academic administrators (e.g., a provost) to instrumental ad ministrators (e.g., a registrar) and that of either kind of administrator to the many varied staff to be found in colleges and universities (e.g., cooks, secretaries, glass blowers, study counselors, accountants, and many other categories of workers). We might skip this topic entirely and refer the reader to the literature in business ethics, where it is extensively discussed in such chapters as "Rights and Obligations of Employers and Employees"[1] or "The [Business] Organization and the People in It."[2] But because the setting of the relationship of managers to their employees or subordinates (to be sure, the managers, too, are employees) makes a difference, it will be worthwhile to take up briefly some moral principles, with an indication as to how they apply to managing behavior vis-à-vis the managed.

There is nothing surprising about the principles; indeed, one might want to assert that they derive from the claim that everyone, including employees, should be treated as persons. This means that managers should respect the rationality of their subordinates, respect their privacy, and treat them fairly. Where such fundamentals are agreed to, a number of practices follow for the workplace. First, whether or not a contract specifies it, to respect rationality requires giving reasons for significant actions that negatively affect employees, most obviously dismissal, demotion, or other disciplining, including the allocation of less of a salary increase than is normal at the time.* The principle of respecting the rationality of human beings, together with the injunction to treat them fairly, quickly yields the requirement that "due process" be used before steps of this kind are taken, not only so that like cases are treated in a like manner, but so as to assure that the decisions made are appropriate, that is, based neither on erroneous judgments nor on characteristics that are irrelevant to the employee's role as worker. Finally, just as a supervisor's judgments should be based on work-related actions and traits, so to respect a subordinate's privacy is to recognize that there is more to a person than being a worker. And since it is only a person's *work* that is hired, to have management intrude into subordinates' private lives—including ascertaining what they think and what they do when not at work—is justified only to the degree to which it is relevant to their functions as workers in a particular enterprise.

While what is summarized in the preceding paragraph tends to take up more than a couple of hundred pages in books on business ethics, in our context only very limited elaboration is appropriate. To begin with, it is by no means universally conceded that due process ought to be followed when an action is taken that adversely affects an employee. Until quite recently, the doctrine of *employment at will* was very widely maintained, stating that "in the absence of law or contract employers have the right to hire, promote, demote, and fire whomever and whenever they please," without providing reasons, even without having any work-related grounds for what is done.[3] While current thinking has shrunk the population of adherents to this tenet and the prevalence of labor contracts has reduced its applicability, the position has by no means disappeared. It is rooted in the libertarian claim that people have the right to accumulate property and to dispose of it at will, and in the viewpoint that what is here owned is the labor for which the worker is compensated. The worker, at any time, is free to quit, and the employer is free to dismiss. Due process interferes with the freedom of both. In effect, this doctrine maintains that it is not persons who are employed,

---

*A recommendation made by the AAUP (AAUP, 1995, 17) deserves consideration in this wider context. An administrator is advised to provide reasons for nonpromotion only if asked and in writing only if asked in writing—and in any case only confidentially to the candidate. This suggestion rests on the claim that it should be up to candidates to decide how much they should "know" when potential future employers make inquiries about what happened. On the other hand, where dismissal is not involved, giving reasons for negative decisions may well be an appropriate part of an evaluation of employees that aims at improving their performances. In any case, it is never up to a third party to let a wider audience know what some particular employee's shortcomings are thought to be (from Weingartner, 1990, n.6).

but just their labor. The transaction is a freely entered exchanging of property: one person's wages for another's work.

Good arguments have been leveled at the doctrine of employment at will, such as one based on the observation that people's labor is their property in a very different sense from that in which their cars or wallets are.[4] But even if one were successful in fending off all extant assaults on this Friedmanesque position, the fact that the workers in question are employed in colleges and universities bears significantly on this cluster of issues. First, consider that the leading members of IHEs are faculty members who, as was already asserted, are not at all *managed* by their administrators; supervising them is not a matter of telling them what they are to do. Moreover, faculty members are not appointed by administrators, as machinists are by a foreman or personnel office, but by means of a collaborative process that gives faculty colleagues a leading role. In a similar way, the determining of faculty members' compensation often involves members of the professoriate, while disciplining faculty members is seldom left solely to an administrator. And almost never is a member of a faculty dismissed without a process in which other faculty members participate, with a particularly elaborate procedure when tenure is involved. In sum, for significant decisions affecting faculty members, there is due process galore.

True enough, might be a response, but what is the relevance of this fact to the treatment of members of an academic institution's staff? They are not faculty members, with the special competencies and functions of that genre; why should they not be dealt with in the same way as are their brethren in the world of business? But while it is true that at least most staff members do the same kind of work as do the employees in a wide variety of commercial enterprises, they are nevertheless distinguished from them precisely by the fact that "rather than inhabit a downtown office building, the staff works on a campus and lives cheek by jowl with students and, more importantly, with faculty."[5] This fact alone constitutes a strong reason to attenuate some of the distinctions between the two types of employees, faculty and staff.

Academic institutions are not well served by an administrative style that, in the conventional sense, runs a tight ship. Indeed, it is at best unclear what this naval excellence could come to when applied to academic units or to IHEs in their entirety. For such institutions have multiple goals that are not commensurate with each other, and a great deal of independence must be given to the principal actors involved in carrying out these goals. And these prime actors are in turn dependent on staff assistance in many different ways. In short, colleges and universities rely upon the personal initiative and motivation of all of their denizens and on the abilities of members of nearly autonomous units both to work together and to cooperate with other units. All this without an administrative apparatus that exacts such collaboration.

Sharp class distinctions work against the voluntary cohesion needed to get the academy's work done effectively. Since no plausible measures are likely to wipe out such significant differences as degree of authority and level of compensation, it is all the more important not to have an institution make glaring distinctions in the ways in which faculty and staff are treated. While tenure would not seem appropriate for glass blowers in the chemistry laboratory, their relationship to the chemistry faculty and the institution is no doubt fostered if significant decisions about their working lives involve consultative and juridical processes that are to some degree analogous to the way the professoriate is treated. It will not do to have members of an institution's staff dismissed with a day's notice and without much of a reason given, while (nontenured) faculty members are given a year's notice and, if desired, provided with reasons in writing. Because of a need to promote initiative and voluntary collaboration so that the institution will serve well its students and other clients, the pursuit of the good of the institution, in other words, constitutes a reason all of its own for treating members of its staff fairly and as persons, as rational beings.

The same considerations pertain to the matter of respecting the privacy of staff members of colleges and universities. Which characteristics and behavior are relevant to one's role as a worker in some given institution—and therefore subject to the employer's decree—can be interpreted broadly or narrowly. For obvious reasons, some automobile companies, for example, prohibit their employees from owning cars other than the brand they produce, though that fact has no bearing on their prowess on the assembly line. Others don't care how employees come to work, as long as they come and do a good job. Analogously, companies differ greatly in what they believe they must know about their employees, with either very tight or quite tenuous arguments supporting such claims. With respect to such continua, most academic institutions tend to be very liberal in their interpretations as to what is to remain as a faculty member's private life. The facts that account for this are such that for all practical purposes, IHEs do not have much choice in the matter. It is simply the case that the academy attracts people whose natural bent is to diverge from conventional patterns of behavior. Since acceptable administrative measures will not much affect such behavior, an institution must either refrain from recruiting from the full pool of the academically qualified or tolerate a certain amount of eccentricity, thus broadening the realm of the private as compared with most business organizations. Such toleration is reinforced by the fact that faculty members must be given considerable autonomy in their professional roles to be able to do their work, a policy that is not readily compatible with close monitoring in other spheres of behavior.

Once again, to assume a less lenient position with respect to the private spheres of members of an IHE's staff than pertains to the faculty (when not directly related to the work assigned) is to sharpen class distinctions. Once again, given the looseness of its organization, a college or university is not well served in carrying out its complex mission by exacerbating inevitable differences in status and treatment of those who must collaborate to accomplish those goals.

II. Supervising the Faculty: To Do and Let Be

It was convenient to begin with a discussion of the administration of an IHE's staff, since we can now say that in administrators' relationships to faculty members, the principles that are applicable there hold as well. To be sure, as has already been suggested, they constitute only a kind of floor, for the related reasons of the sort of institution a college or university is and the professional status of the faculty. In our tradition, which goes back to the Middle Ages, it is conceded—sometimes reluctantly and never unanimously—that these responsibilities are best discharged by institutions that are quite autonomous, going about their various businesses without direction and interference from outside their walls. Even when—as tends to be the case in state institutions—certain goals are set from the outside, the institution is expected to reach them in its own way.[6] It would be ironical if society granted autonomy to the institution but the administrators of the institution then took it away from those who do most of its work. If the institution is "free" because its professional nature gives it (and not the lay world) the competence to perform the pedagogical and research functions that are expected of it, so must the professionals within it—those who actually engage in pedagogical and scholarly activities—be free to go about their business. If no demands are made of the institution to espouse or impart some particular viewpoints or doctrines because it is held that knowledge is most effectively sought and passed on where discussion is free and unfettered, so must this liberty be passed on to the pertinent actors within the college or university. Faculty and students must not only be free from so blatant shackles as censorship, but free, as well, from the more subtle coercion of official institutional viewpoints.[7] Finally, as has been asserted before, given the professional standing of faculty members who are not "managed" like workers on a factory floor, decisions about the conditions of their employment—including that of whether to be employed—must centrally involve peers.

These are essential principles that must be in effect in an IHE; they, above all, distinguish academic institutions from most, if not all, other institutions in our society. And if they were the only sort there in operation, the only function for specifically academic administrators would be *laisser aller*, to let be. But we know that colleges and universities are not mere collectivities—educational or research bazaars—and that it is academic administrators who bear the responsibility for their transformation into conglomerates that fulfill *institutional* goals and meet the obligations owed to students, to sponsors of research, and to society at large. Accordingly, academic administrators have the complex duty both to do and to let be. Generically, that paradox is best explicated by means of another: regard academic administration as the supervision of faculty self-governance. And, to stay at the same level of abstraction, this comes above all to exercising the power of initiative and to fulfilling the function of quality control, both functions supported by substantial control over the purse.

We have already seen in our discussion of teaching[8] that academic administrators are responsible for the organization of the faculty into groupings—schools, departments—that enable them not just to teach courses, but to provide students with the educational programs included in the institution's repertory. Since no set of courses or requirements is suitable for all time, administrators must see to it as well that agencies exist to monitor an academic institution's curricula and see to it that there are agencies that develop new pedagogies at all levels. This latter task is not simply a matter of pushing a "start" button and waiting for whatever might result from some committee's deliberation, but requires constant questioning, probing, and prodding. Finally, the members of academic institutions must know how well they are doing and not fall prey to the assumption that they are doing well because it is they who are the doers. While the impetus to undertake what has come to be called "assessment" largely came from outside colleges and universities, determining what has and has not been accomplished by means of an educational program is a necessary step in any effort to improve it. As the agents responsible for seeing to it that the institution is accomplishing its goals, academic administrators must see to it that ways are devised for determining whether and to what degree that is the case and put what is learned to use.

III. Maintaining a Competent Faculty

The evaluation of the teaching of individual faculty members—already stressed for a number of significant reasons—must come to play a particular role in the new era in which there is no mandated retirement age. On the whole, IHEs have been most diffident about taking action with respect to unqualified faculty members. But prior to the time at which the grant of indefinite tenure became a contract for life, it was a matter of relatively rare chance that a faculty would harbor a tenured member who was simply not qualified for the job he or she held. Committees and administrators make occasional mistakes; unusual circumstances in someone's life—in health or family conditions, say—can have the kind of devastating effect that reduces a once able person to incompetency. Even though colleges and universities tend to act only in the most flagrant and conspicuous cases, such as rampant alcoholism, perhaps not all that much harm was done under a dispensation that required faculty members to retire by the age of seventy or earlier.

Now, however, the potentiality of incompetency has been introduced into academic institutions in a systemic way. There is nothing accidental about aging. And if it is not inevitable that the ability to perform a given job then comes to wane, the likelihood increases markedly. Moreover, such declining, particularly if mental rather than physical, is not necessarily accompanied by an awareness of that fact or by a willingness to draw the consequences for one's life. The situation just described, accordingly, is sufficient to require academic administrators to initiate systematic reviews of tenured faculty.[9]

It is argued that such reviews are wasteful of faculty time because they do not or would not lead to more faculty dismissals than do the rarely used procedures for removing a faculty member for unprofessional conduct. Since any review procedure must centrally involve faculty peers, the claim that they are futile is clearly rooted in the observation that professionals more generally have proven to be most deficient in their abilities to police themselves. But required post-tenure reviews taking place at specific colleges or universities must be distinguished from committees of physicians or attorneys in some jurisdiction acting—or not—on the sporadic complaints about a fellow professional brought before them. The context is institutional, and the chief distinguishing ingredient is the academic administrator, speaking as the conscience of the institution and representing its clients.

In short, the task of academic administrators is not limited to setting up post-tenure reviews, but to assure that they are effective in revealing what is the case about the performance of a faculty member. Effective and fair. Just as it is possible to respect the sphere in which a faculty member is appropriately autonomous in the course of evaluations that are made before tenure is accorded, so is it possible after tenure has been achieved. The fact that on rare occasions colleagues cannot agree whether someone's very eccentric work is highly original or incompetent does not undermine the fact that in the overwhelming majority of cases, judgments of competency do not raise special intellectual difficulties.

In our discussion of post-tenure reviews, we have considered the most drastic of cases, because we began it with the elimination of mandatory retirement and the specter of senility. But for most faculty members, post-tenure reviews would begin when they are in their thirties, and one would expect findings anywhere from excellence to incompetence, with the latter indeed rare. Moreover, although we began with worries about teaching, the evaluations here envisaged should be concerned with all aspects of the roles of faculty members, including research and service to the institution. These reviews, then, alert administrators to the need or opportunity for different kinds of actions vis-à-vis members of their faculty. On the one hand, not yet drastic problems may be uncovered regarding which one or another kind of remedial action can be taken. On the other, abilities and interests may be revealed that enable an administrator to enlist a faculty member for some special role useful to the academic community. In sum, when looked at more broadly, a scheme of post-tenure reviews must be regarded as a part of the strategy that informs academic administrators about what and how they are doing in the guidance of their institution.

IV. Research Integrity

The stress, in the discussion of this section, has been on teaching, because it is a significant duty of academic administrators to see to it that, as its clients, the institution's students are well served. One might think that because, as researchers, faculty members resemble nothing so much as independent contractors, academic administrators have no significant supervisory role—beyond the encouragement of excellence, as previously discussed. The clients of researchers, after all, are not inside the IHE; rather, society, out there, is always a client or some larger or smaller subsection thereof—especially the collectivity of investigators in the same field. Often there is a more specific client as well, and in the natural sciences almost always. These are organizations that put up some or all of the money needed to carry out a particular project, most frequently a governmental agency—such as the National Science Foundation or the National Institutes of Health, created specifically to support research—but it could also be a nongovernmental (not-for- profit) foundation or, particularly in the life sciences and in clinical areas, corporations that are in business to make money. But whoever these extramural clients, it would be plausible to hold that it is only they who have supervisory roles. Society will oversee by rewarding with praise and granting royalties or by disparaging the work done and making its publication difficult or impossible. When pleased, those specific clients and their brethren will go on to support additional projects, perhaps on a larger scale; when dissatisfied, they will withhold support and make carrying on research difficult or impossible. The market, so goes this line of thought, is all the supervision that is needed.

Nevertheless, there are at least two additional issues—besides the matter of rewarding quality—where academic administrators must perform a supervisory function. Thanks to widespread discussions in recent years—and not always pleasant ones—the first issue to be taken up has received the widely used label of "research integrity." To get at what is meant by this trait, near synonyms, such as *honesty* or *rectitude*, don't help much, nor does it make much sense to try to spell out all the right things one should do to maintain such integrity, as one engages in research in a huge range of fields. Thus, the most effective way of conveying what is meant by this integrity is to characterize its absence and to define research *mis*conduct instead. While no formula is likely to be universally agreed upon, a succinct statement by an agency of the National Academy will serve our purposes: "Misconduct in science is defined as fabrication, falsification, or plagiarism, in proposing, performing, or reporting research," with the further explications: "Fabrication is making up data or results, falsification is changing data or results, and plagiarism is using the ideas and words of another person without giving appropriate credit."[10]

Agreed that these are the crimes "that violate traditional values of the research enterprise and that may be detrimental to the research process."[11] But why should the problems that are inevitably generated when these ethical rules are violated not just be a matter of concern for those directly involved, researcher and client? There are several aspects to the answer. To begin with, the researcher *is* a part of a college or university and not really a fully independent operator. And just as the reputations of institutions benefit from the praise and prizes bestowed on members of their faculties, so they suffer when members of their faculties are censured for misconduct in research. Indeed, when research is funded by an outside agency, governmental or private, the practice is not to dispense the funds directly to the researcher, but rather to the institution, for use by him or her, on the assumption that the institution will exercise some oversight. And with respect to our issue of research integrity, that makes a good deal of sense, since for many reasons, client agencies are in no position to determine what goes on at many distant places where they support research. Nor would (or should) a college or university want such agencies to intervene in its own affairs. When the client is society at large or an amorphous group of consumers of some type of research, individuals or professional groups might be able to raise suspicions or even provide evidence—as for plagiarism, for example—but except for rare censures by professional organizations, there is little that people outside a researcher's institution can do about transgressors or suspected transgressors.

That the researchers' institutions must themselves assume responsibility for research integrity in their domains is underlined by the fact that it is very tricky to distinguish between morally culpable violations of the principles of research, on the one hand, and error, carelessness, or even incompetence, on the other. After all, "[m]isconduct in science does not include errors of judgment, errors in recording, selection, or analysis of data; differences in opinions involving the interpretation of data; or misconduct unrelated to the research process," as is stated as the very next sentence after the brief National Academy definition given above.[12] It can be difficult to determine whether a piece of work was done sloppily or whether there was intentional cheating, especially in research undertakings that are both complex and carried on in an atmosphere of fierce competition. If anyone can cope with the problems raised by research integrity, it is the institution at which the research is conducted. And since someone must, *it* must.

But if IHEs have an obligation, so do their academic administrators, whose duties, typically, combine both doing and letting be. Details on how to cope with the problems raised by research integrity are not appropriate here, but an outline will reveal some of the roles to be played by administrators.[13] The best way to cope, to begin with, is to try to avoid having to deal with actual research misconduct by preventing its occurrence. We have already taken up one way in which academic administrators can serve this cause: they can reduce the perceived, if desperate, need to cheat by reducing the pressure to produce, by stressing quality of research over quantity.[14]

But there is an equally important second role, and that is to counteract a widespread form of wishful thinking of academics that has many of them believe that there is much that students and junior colleagues will somehow pick up by rubbing shoulders with their elders, without anyone's ever needing to *say* anything. Although the formula stating what constitutes academic misconduct may be short, it needs to be interpreted and made specific for the many different fields of research, where, in each of them, it also generates ambiguities and hard cases. Academic administrators must insist that departments, laboratories, and research groups spell out the rules appropriate to their work, in effect setting explicit standards for research integrity. Moreover, all of these units must make those documents the bases for discussions among themselves and with their students. As a result of such educational activity, no one accused of research misconduct should plausibly be able to plead that he or she did not know that what was done was wrong. Administrators initiate; faculty members execute. But the former hasn't happened unless the latter has: A memorandum to all departmental chairpersons does not initiate unless the desired educational processes are actually undertaken and remain ongoing activities in all relevant units.

The third role of academic administrators is to set up "procedures for soliciting, examining, and settling complaints" concerning misconduct in research.[15] While, again, the stress is on setting up and, one might add, on sustaining, each component of this complex task has its own requirements. To concoct *procedures* for soliciting allegations of research malfeasance is the least of it. It is vastly more difficult to engender the dual belief in members of the institution that well founded (though not necessarily incontrovertibly so) whistle-blowing is appropriate and will not be punished, while frivolous or malicious whistle-blowing will be censured. This is ultimately a matter of the ethos of a place and, it will be argued, academic administrators have a role in shaping it. That faculty members have the primary role in examining charges of misconduct in research would seem obvious, since only among fellow practitioners of a craft will the knowledge be found that can sort out the issues in any particular case. Again, the administrator's task is to initiate and to select with tact the teams that will scrutinize a particular case: collectively possessing the requisite knowledge without harboring investigators who are predisposed to take one side or the other.

Finally, there is the matter of acting on what an investigation has revealed. Importantly, this includes preserving the good name of someone who was found to have done no wrong. Difficult though that is, since academic institutions are not very good at maintaining confidentiality, it has proven more difficult still to find appropriate responses when investigations show that there was misconduct. To be sure, the repertory of punishments of IHEs is limited—"[t]hey cannot imprison."[16] Nevertheless, the tendency, in the academy, to think in terms of all or nothing—dismissal (using appropriate procedures) or no chastisement at all—indicates a failure either of imagination or of nerve. Intermediate forms of punishment must surely be resorted to since unless there is significant punishment for significant transgressions, all the institutional churning about research integrity will have been a charade. Again, it falls to academic administrators to help faculty groups transcend a timidity that is rooted in feelings of there-but-for-the-grace-of-God-go-I and to ensure that institutional obligations with respect to research integrity are met.

V. Research and Profit

Academic administrators have to exercise further supervisory functions with respect to faculty research and research-related activities that are in some ways even more difficult than those pertaining to research integrity. The relationship between scientific discoveries and their utilization in for-profit ventures has given rise, especially during the last two decades or so, to ever more perplexing issues about what does and does not constitute conflict of interest and what are and what are not appropriate activities for members of a university's faculty or, for that matter, of a university's administration. This is a big topic, to which an entire volume in this series is devoted, a topic that does not lend itself to succinct summary here.[17] But it is possible and appropriate to give a sufficient account of these issues so as to show why they are pertinent to the theme of the moral dimensions of academic administration.

The cluster of issues with which we are here concerned is rooted in the fact that research in the sciences may lead to products and services that can be profitable, even highly profitable, to those who produce and market them. This is hardly news; the presocratic philosopher Thales was said to have cornered the olive market on the basis of his superior understanding of the relation of meteorology to agriculture. Indeed, the likelihood of profit is already implicit when we note that universities are given a special status in part because the research that is undertaken there will benefit society. After all, those benefits are very seldom conferred directly—in that one gains simply by *knowing* what has been discovered—but require some enterprise to convert what has come to be known into a product or service that members of society find useful or desirable. These mediating enterprises, to be sure, do not have to be profit making; a government, for example, leaning on university research, could itself manufacture a vaccine that immunizes against some disease and dispense it to its population. But, with few exceptions, things do not work that way in the society we live in; for us, private businesses and corporations are the engines that convert scientific discoveries into benefits that can, so to speak, be consumed by society.

We can thus begin with a simple picture. The IHE faculty members engage in research, supported by their own institutions and by governmental or private agencies that are in business *pro bono publico*. When projects are completed, the findings are made public, at meetings open to all interested listeners and, above all, in publications available to everyone who can pay what they cost or who has access to a library. Some listeners and readers will have the understanding, initiative, and resources to try to utilize what they have learned and will make a product in which people might be interested. Some of these entrepreneurs will succeed and give the public something it wants, while the developer makes money. Although things were surely never quite that simple, let us nevertheless think of that picture as portraying the good old days. Old, because it is a depiction of a mythical past; good, because, with respect to research, the academic institutions—and the people within them—are doing precisely what they should be: working for the benefit of the society that supports them.

In several different and significant ways, the current real world differs from this idyllic one. (1) Faculty researchers, in addition to publishing their findings, may apply for and receive patents based on their work, from which income may be derived. (2) Alternatively, rather than the individual faculty member, the academic institution may become the owner of such a patent. (3) Instead of receiving support for research from a governmental agency or private foundation, the support might come from a corporation, with the understanding that the firm has privileged access to research results. (4) In addition to teaching and engaging in research at their institutions, faculty members may use their knowledge and skills in the service of for-profit organizations, either as consultants or by working for them under some other arrangement. (5) Instead of merely working for some for-profit company that is engaged in work that is related to his or her research area, a faculty member might be an owner of such a business or the owner, with the former possibly including a managerial role and the latter necessarily so. (6) Finally, a university itself might use some of its capital and such other resources as space to create a for-profit corporation that utilizes the research of some of its faculty members.

Now these different practices, all of them in operation at some American IHEs and many carried on at a large number of them, modify—indeed compromise—in different ways and to varying degrees the proper relationship between academic institutions and their denizens and society. If the individual faculty or university patent holder, to begin with (1) and (2), uses the income derived therefrom to support further research, one might regard the profits from research as so allocated as to provide further benefits for society. If the individual faculty member takes the proceeds derived from a patent as personal income, then work that is supported by society is wrongly used to enrich an individual. (The fact that faculty writers of profitable textbooks or faculty artists' remunerative commissions have always gone unchallenged, as Donald Kennedy points out, does not change the fact that work done "on the job" and with support of the institution is wrongly diverted to private gain.[18] It just makes it harder for academic administrators to be both right and equitable.) If a university takes its profits from patents to raise the salaries of administrators or to recruit better football players, that institution is equally remiss, unless it can be persuasively argued that either of these expenditures benefits society.

When (3) the condition for research support from business sources is access to results prior to publication, the rules of the game are bent. When such support blocks the public dissemination of some or all of the research findings, the rules are most seriously violated, in that the research benefits are channeled to a single recipient. It will not do to say that, after all, the underwriters get no more than they paid for, since their contributions do not extend to the creation and support of the institution that makes any particular project possible. The university setting is *used*, so to speak, as a private laboratory.

Faculty researchers, instead of working for some pharmaceutical house in the university laboratory, may (4) put their abilities at its disposal off campus, as a consultant or part-time employee. This exceedingly widespread practice rests on the simple claim that what faculty members do in their free time is their own business. But two minutes' worth of reflection[19] shows this simplicity to be most deceptive. How much of faculty members' time is free, given that employment by an IHE does not specify a certain number of hours of work? But suppose one accepts the widely used answer that faculty members may accept outside work for the equivalent of one day a week; then deeper questions intrude. Since the work done off campus is not notably different from that done in the university laboratory—as would be the case with Kennedy's "innocent" example of science professor as part-time gourmet chef[20]—it is easy to see how fulfilling the intellectual demands of off-campus work can become part of the on-campus research activity. Neatly separating one day from the other six hardly describes what actually transpires where a faculty member's research would thus be prompted, wholly or in part, by the consultant's needs.

It is difficult for faculty researchers to resist the temptation to solve problems that confront them as consultants on university time, so to speak—and thus increase their value as consultants. It is well-nigh impossible to keep separate university work from company work when (5) the professor is also an officer and part owner of a research-related company. And when (6) the university itself is the entrepreneur, it is the case of the pope himself selling indulgences, in that it appears to make legitimate what is essentially a corrupting practice. In their different ways—one retail, the other wholesale—these practices place the values of business, with profit as the controlling goal, into the center of an IHE. Even without attractive distractions, it may be hard to determine which research programs are likely to make the most significant contributions to a field and to act on that judgment. Given the expectation that *this* work is likely to be lucrative to researchers and their institutions, it is difficult to imagine that *that* work will be pursued, no matter what its scientific merit. When one mixes water and vinegar, the resulting liquid will have the taste of the latter. Similarly, it is no revelation to note that the profit motive is so powerful an incentive wherever it secures a footing it is likely to dominate.

A brief account has been given of some (and only some) of the issues that are raised by different practices that pull research in the academy away from its orientation *pro bono publico*. Derek Bok, among others, has however pointed to a cumulative effect of this commercialization of research. "Universities attract that loyalty of faculty and alumni and, to a degree, the respect of the public precisely because they act for reasons other than money and will not compromise certain values simply to gain immediate monetary rewards. As universities grow more aggressive to turn their activities into cash, their image subtly changes. They appear less and less as a charitable institution seeking truth and serving students and more and more as a huge commercial operation that differs from corporations only because there are no shareholders and no dividends."[21] Without doubt Bok is an astute observer of the scene of higher education, and his views about the loss of respect for academic institutions are certainly seconded by an equally perceptive witness, Donald Kennedy. Both of these retired university presidents, however, tend to treat these changes in ethos as a passage in historical anthropology of academic institutions: that is how the culture of the academy used to be; this is how it is now, with certain consequences for institutions' reputations. But the changes of which a summary account has here been given pertain to the *moral* foundation of IHEs. Given our premises regarding the nature of academic institutions and the reasons society brings them into existence and supports them, many of these practices are just plain wrong. There is much, in short, for academic administrators to do to preserve—or rather get back to—an ethos that is appropriate to the kind of institutions that are the subject of this book.[22]

VI. Creating and Sustaining an Ethos

Conduct post-tenure reviews to maintain a competent faculty; supervise practices that will tend to avert research misconduct; devise means to keep the profit motive reined in. The importance of such duties makes it seem as if academic administration is largely a form of highfalutin police work. And it is true that one aspect of administration is a kind of sentry duty, with the primary goal of preventing wrongdoing and the secondary one of punishing it when it occurs. But we know that civil society could not function—*pace* Hobbes—if order and purposiveness

depended solely or even largely on the vigilance and power of the police. Instead, society depends on the benignity of the habits and desires
of the vast majority of its members, instilled and cultivated via numerous routes, from family to school, to a large array of institutions and
practices. Similarly, academic administrators depend on the background and training of their faculty to confine their watchdog activities
to a concern with a limited number of sinners who are exceptions to the
norm.

But however desirable, the maintenance of an institution that is relatively free of misconduct is only background to the positive accomplishment of a college's or university's specific goals, in the style, moreover,
and expressive of the values of that particular academic institution. For
that to happen, in a world in which the leading "workers" are not managed, academic administrators must not only exercise leadership, but
also contribute to the ethos of the institution.

In prior chapters and in this one, we have in effect taken up many of
the activities of which administrative leadership in the academy consists, mostly without so labeling them. But leading calls for the articu-
lating of goals, the selecting and organizing of the people who will accomplish them; the initiating and guiding of processes of change; and it
calls for activities that assure, in many different contexts, that the institution's standards of quality are met. But just as successful policing depends on a prevalence of salutary habits in the population being over-
seen, so academic leadership is effective only in a context in which
those who are to be led are predisposed to follow, indeed are by and
large inclined to act appropriately without the need of being led. Much
of that predisposition is a function of the nature and drawing power of
an institution's ethos.

An ethos, of course, consists of the sorts of things that are normally
done at a place and finds its expression in an institution's rules that are
explicitly stated, in the practices that people follow even though they
are never formulated, as well as in customs that are *not* observed in that
place. But the ethos of a college or university is perhaps expressed
even more distinctively not in *what* is done there, but *how* things are
done. Do people work to serve—the faculty to educate students, the
registrar to enable students to exercise their course choices, administrators to facilitate the work of the faculty—or do they work to suit
their own convenience and to make a buck? What degree of striving do
people expect from each other and what degree do they tend to get?
Then there is what is sometimes called "tone." Do people tend to be
civil to each other; are they, in general, kind and generous, or are they
more likely to be brusque, harsh, and niggardly? Do those who have
authority over others usually accompany the expression of their direc-

tives with reasons and explanations, or can they be expected simply to convey or even bark their orders? Of course, by no means are all such continua characterized by one pole that is clearly the desirable one. Thus, for example, institutions also vary in the degree to which people take themselves and their ideas seriously—to the point of solemnity—or the degree to which a certain distance, even lightheartedness, is likely to be maintained. Many other institutional traits can be added to these, with some of them of course pertaining more specifically to pedagogic and research practices and attitudes, while others characterize an institution more generally. Were one to spell all of this out, the ethos of an institution would then be described by its location on the many continua of the sort of samples that have here been given. Finally, one can assess all of these traits for their potency, that is, for the depth to which they are ingrained in the institution and the magnitude of the sway they exercise over its denizens.

All this is well enough, a reader may respond, perhaps what has been said points to a way in which an institution's ethos might be characterized. But what is it doing in a discussion of what academic administrators are supposed to do? That ethos, whatever it is, evolves over time, is constantly shaped and modified by innumerable interacting factors and forces, both inside and outside the institution, many of them well-nigh invisible. That reference to the sophomore history student's favorite historical causes—factors and forces—conveys that an ethos is held to be something that happens to institutions as a consequence of complex and, if DeMaistre and Burke are right, essentially unanalyzable processes. On this view, individuals come and go, and if they have an effect at all on an institution's ethos, it is not because that is what they intended. Moreover, should there indeed be a causal relation between the actions of a person and the ethos of the institution, it is unlikely to be discernable, or at best it becomes known only in retrospect.

While there is some truth in that account, it surely much exaggerates the mysteriousness of the formation of an ethos. With respect to the issues that here concern us most, it should be granted, first, that while individuals may consciously aim at modifying an ethos, no activities, exempting drastic cases, will assure that they actually do so and, second, that one is not likely to know when the actions of an individual have actually modified an ethos until at least some time after those activities have taken place.* What cannot be conceded, however, is that the ac-

---

*An amusing small example from my own experience: During a bad budget year, when I was dean at Northwestern, next to no money was available for faculty salary increases. Since this fact precluded giving the customary merit raises and since the annual teaching awards were also given in the form of raises

tions of individuals might not significantly contribute to the formation of an institution's ethos (whether or not that is known), that they will not play a significant role when those "factors and forces" are analyzed with their component causal elements.

Moreover, if we do not know how to guarantee success, we certainly have convictions as to how we might try to shape the ethos of our institutions, just as we have many well founded beliefs as to how we should raise our children without thereby being assured of success. Indeed, just as whatever we do persistently in our homes is likely to have an influence on the kind of persons our children become—so intended or not—so persistent actions and expressions of attitudes of leading academic administrators is likely to shape an institution's ethos.*

Because the right kind of ethos, and one that is sufficiently rooted to be compelling, is such a support in the accomplishment of the goals of an IHE, we are once again in the position where *because we can, we ought*. Academic administrators, accordingly, must act on the insight that their respect for faculty is likely to breed faculty respect for administration; that their respect for students will help to engender faculty and staff respect for students. Administrative support for the central enterprises of the institution will tend to generate greater effort devoted to those tasks by faculty and staff. These are merely some examples of types of deeds and attitudes, expressible in small matters and in large, which, if steadfastly exhibited and enacted, will become part of the ethos of a college or a university. Academic administrators, for better or for worse, are role models.

And when for better, academic administering does not largely deteriorate into academic policing. Instead, the institution's ethos serves as a kind of invisible hand that makes it possible for an academic institution's many and varied professionals to accomplish the institution's goals without being managed like workers on an assembly line.

(rather than one-time prizes), I decided to omit awarding them as well. When that fact became known, I was visited by a small delegation of respectful but very determined students who wanted me to know how wrong it was for me not to honor this hallowed and important Northwestern tradition. What the students had not known was the fact that I had initiated these teaching awards the year after I came to Northwestern, just three or four years earlier.

*These may be extreme examples, but I have no doubt (if not much evidence) that the significant differences in ethos between Columbia and Harvard Universities are importantly attributable to their two long-reigning presidents. Nicholas Murray Butler's authoritarian personality and style is undoubtedly coresponsible for the fact that Columbia is a more hierarchical and administration-driven university than the more faculty-centered Harvard, which was ushered into the twentieth century by Charles Eliot, with a very different personality and working philosophy.

Notes

1. Beauchamp and Bowie, 1993, chapter 5, 253–363; also see chapter 6, 364–441.
2. Shaw and Barry, 1992, part III, 261–476.
3. Werhane, 1985, 262; what follows depends on Werhane's discussion.
4. That argument and others are to be found in Werhane, 1985.
5. Weingartner, 1996, xiv; what follows is an elaboration of the points there made.
6. See, in this series of Issues in Academic Ethics, De George, 1997, especially 10–13 and 53–68, for elaboration and justification.
7. See, in this series of Issues in Academic Ethics, Simon, 1994, 19–39, for his development and defense of the concept of "critical neutrality."
8. See chapter 4, section II.
9. See De George, 1997, 39–43, for a good discussion of post-tenure review with which I am in substantial agreement.
10. Scientific Responsibility, 1992, 27.
11. Scientific Responsibility, 1992, 28.
12. Scientific Responsibility, 1992, 27.
13. The discussion here leans particularly on the succinct formulations in Davis, 1990, especially 7–8, though there is broad agreement among those who have written on what universities should be doing with respect to research integrity.
14. See chapter 5, section III.
15. Davis, 1990, 7.
16. Davis, 1990, 7.
17. The book is Bowie, 1994, a volume that includes an essay by the author, as well as extensive readings on all aspects of the topic of university-business partnerships. For a brief but rich account of the many types of issues that are confronted by faculty members and their institutions—pertaining to anything from various types of consulting to assuming managerial roles in for-profit enterprises—see Kennedy, 1997, chapter 9, "To Reach Beyond the Walls," 241–264.
18. Kennedy, 1997, 244.
19. Helped along by Kennedy's astute discussion: Kennedy, 1997, chapter 9, *passim.*
20. Kennedy, 1997, 250.
21. Bok, 1991, 120.
22. For the expression of a view similar to that put forward here, together with some advice as to what to do, see Wade, 1984.

Chapter 7

Two Practices

The preceding chapters have dealt quite broadly with some of the moral dimensions of academic administration. But moral issues arise in the course of many of the day-to-day doings of administrators, so that it will be worthwhile to look at some of these, pertaining to two different practices that occupy academic administrators at every IHE. Our first example is concerned with the setting of salaries of faculty members; the second example looks at personnel decisions, specifically the crucial decision as to whether tenure should or should not be granted.

I. Some Moral Dimensions of the Determination of Faculty Salaries

While IHEs vary considerably in the manner and degree to which faculty members participate in the setting of their colleagues' salaries (if they do at all), academic administrators are almost always the leaders in the assignment of faculty salaries and usually have the final say. A significant moral dimension of this aspect of the work of administrators might seem to be quite straightforward: heed the call of distributive justice, and give equal pay for equal work, considering both the quantity and the quality of that labor, and paying more for more (and better) work and less for less. Straightforward, indeed, and perhaps defensible as an ideal, though in utopia this dictum would at least have to contend with Marx's "from each according to his ability; to each according to his need." But in any case, it is not without problems in application.

Take first the matter of seniority. It is the practice—and expectation—that people who have served longer receive higher pay. Experience may improve the quality of the work done, but surely not always. Indeed, improved quality over time is probably seldom thought of as a

significant justification for this salary policy. The reasons for this practice are more likely to include the fact that we generally live in an infla-
tionary environment, that for a long time span the needs of maturing
persons increase, and that it would seriously disrupt individual and institutional lives if every year salaries were set totally anew. But in an
important sense, to increase compensation with time served does not violate our rule of equity. In principle, equity is reestablished when one
considers an entire career. Thus, while at any given time, one person
will receive higher pay for the same work than a more junior person,
that (now) junior person can look forward to being treated in the same
way in the future. Thus, when one takes time into consideration—and
assuming a generous ceteris paribus—attention to seniority in one's salary policy does not violate the rule of giving equal pay for equal work.*

Second, determining what is more or less work, quantitatively and
qualitatively, may be difficult and imprecise, but equity requires one to
do one's best to make the assessments. Start with teaching. Even measuring quantities has its difficulties. To be sure, within a given framework, what is more and what is less can be established reasonably well.
But the frameworks themselves are problematical, as is reflected in the
rather unsystematic variations in standard teaching loads and the inter-
minable squabbles about them. It is these standards, accordingly, that
need from time to time to be reexamined, especially as modes of teaching change. As regards the quality of teaching, we have already discussed the rewarding of excellent teaching as an inducement.[1] Our current context, however, suggests that for the sake of equity, the results of
the evaluation of teaching be made part of an institution's salary policy.

One might, additionally, inquire about the relationship between quantity and quality. Often, there certainly is such a connection, if what is
measured is time and effort. While, for some, talent is a substitute,
working harder and longer at teaching may well result in more and better learning by students. But the economics of IHEs place a limit on
what is possible in practice. That many students must be taught and this
many faculty members are available to do the teaching. Faculty deployment is thus likely to embody a compromise between an ideal quality of
teaching (perhaps calling for much effort dedicated to very small
classes) and the necessity of teaching of a given number of students.

When one turns to research, institutional needs do not impose an
analogous constraint. As was argued above,[2] the world needs more good
research; not just more research. Bad institutional habits perpetuate the

---

*Things are certainly not equal for nonregular faculty. The growing use of·
part-time and other nontenure track faculty, already discussed in chapter 5, section II, will again be taken up in this chapter, below.

stress on quantity. It is, however, perfectly compatible with the demands of equity to require that more of a faculty member's time and effort is devoted to the pursuit of research quality, even at the expense of quantity, and to have a salary policy that allocates rewards accordingly.

Better or more work justifies higher compensation, given our dictum of distributive justice; two phenomena of the real world, however, lead to distortions of that principle, particularly at more ambitious colleges and universities. The first is related to quality of research but is not identical to it. The work certain people do gives them considerable visibility; their presence on a faculty contributes to the reputation of their institution. No doubt, the research such "stars" produce—and it is almost always research rather than teaching prowess that creates celebrities— has to be substantial in quantity and quality. But usually there is also something else that is not simply more of the same. That star professor is like the outfielder who hits fifty-five home runs a season, as compared with the shortstop who seldom misses a play, bats .285, but not very often for extra bases. To have a good team, both are needed, but the home run hitting outfielder brings in the crowds. And so with a scholar of renown: someone whose work is in fashion, wins prizes, is noted by a larger public. Such a person is likely to attract students (though directly only graduate students), may be helpful in recruiting of faculty in related fields, and may contribute to the "rating" of the institution, which, in turn, contributes to its thriving in various ways. Whether and how much that happens depends not only on the institutional context (one celebrity in a mediocre institution will do little), but also on the genuineness of the grounds for the celebrity (clever self-promotion may be an alternative), as well as on the way the possessor of the fame uses it.

As stars, then, faculty members often do make special contributions to the welfare of academic institutions; and because that can be thought of as being a form of "more work," they are entitled to higher compensation. However, instead of being at the top of the scale, the pay of these celebrities is often in a stratosphere high above it. It is usually propelled to these heights in the course of bidding wars that add to high salaries support and other perquisites that are available to no one else, including significant reductions in teaching duties, in some cases down to having no such obligations at all.

Many an institution's budget can afford a certain number of celebrities, considering both salary and other support. Moreover, many a faculty will accept a limited number of such stars in their midst, especially if they regard the fame as earned and as efficacious in advancing the institution. There is little doubt, however, that the practice of garnishing a faculty with stars can be and is greatly overdone, a product of academic administrators' losing sight of the central goals of their institutions.[3]

First, it can be a serious misallocation of funds: an investment in glamour with uncertain results rather than in more mundane but more certain teaching and research power. (The team does need that shortstop.) Second, and perhaps still more significantly, an excessive use of stars distorts the structure of incentives at an institution. Fame comes to be regarded as more important than solidity of scholarship and *direct* contributions to the missions of the institution, a distortion that is amplified by the fact that the larger the number of stars, the more probable that there are counterfeits among them. Worse than outsized salaries are significant reductions of teaching duties: academic administrators are not credible when stressing the importance of teaching if they excuse whom they prize most from that crucial activity. Finally, the star system creates divisions in a faculty and is destructive of faculty morale and of the kind of community on which the satisfactory functioning of a college or university depends.

It is of course because there is such a lively market for them that academic celebrities are so munificently rewarded. The market, however, plays a role in all academic appointments; and this general phenomenon constitutes the second real-world fact that compels modifications of the principle of equal work for equal pay. It is simply the case, everything else being equal, that anesthesiologists are paid more than pathologists; instructors of accounting get more than those who teach organizational behavior; professors of economics receive higher salaries than those of French literature. There is no single explanation for these and many other variations in salary scale, though the law of supply and demand is surely an ingredient in all of them.

The effects of the market on faculty salaries cannot be wished away, but, in two ways, they can and ought to be mitigated by academic administrators, both in order to edge a bit closer to the requirement of distributive justice and to contribute to the cohesiveness of the institution. The first is to reduce participation in bidding wars. Such contests open the doors wide to the market and invite it into the institution. While the process begins with stars or would-be stars, it affects much of the rest of the faculty, above all by engendering the belief that only by waving an outside offer can one get a significant salary increase. When true, and it often is, this also amounts to shirking the responsibility for determining what the institution itself should value.

The second way to mitigate some of the ways in which the effects of the market distort an equitable distribution of salaries is to recognize that while one cannot long get away with paying less for a given service than the minimum that is determined by the market, one can certainly pay more. It not only makes for a more equitable distribution of salaries, but it also contributes to institutional cohesion when the salary floor is raised where there are sharp market differentials among groups of faculty who live in daily juxtaposition with each other and whose work is essentially the same.*

But this mention of salary floors reminds us that there is more to the moral dimension of salary policy than the dictates of distributive justice. After all, such equity would be served where everyone who is doing the same work—and a lot of it—is paid a pittance. And the market, at least for the foreseeable future, makes exceedingly low compensation possible, especially for nonregular faculty. We have already discussed the need to limit the proportion of such faculty with inferior status;[4] now we must comment on their remuneration.

The differences in salaries that tend to be paid to regular (tenure track) faculty and to various types of nonregular instructors are considerable. It is at times said that this gap is not inequitable, because the contributions that lecturers make are limited: They are called upon only to teach and are expected neither to engage in research nor to participate in the governance of the institution. Whether the differences between the two types of salary mirror faithfully the differences in duties and contributions may be difficult to determine, but when administrators actually try to do so, rather than just mumble a self-serving formula, the result is likely to be greater equity. Moreover, it is certainly the case that experience counts for much less for nonregular faculty, without there being reasons for differences in average increases besides the institution's desire to save money.

And it is to save money that many of the nonregular faculty are employed. Within limits, appropriately so, since for certain teaching roles the use of nonregular faculty is compatible with the effective achievement of institutional goals. Three general observations, however, are here in order. First, institutions must resist the temptation to exploit particular classes of people who have few if any alternatives to accepting whatever they are offered. Spouses—more often than not wives—of faculty members would be one example, especially in relatively isolated geographic settings. It is not necessarily right to do what the market permits.

---

*One can certainly argue that these salary expenditures not required by the market do have a bearing on the market—most obviously in the context of for-profit businesses. Money so spent either reduces profits or is not available to be spent on something else that might contribute to greater productivity—in either case a disadvantage, relative to competitors. But it is a disadvantage only if those higher salaries don't themselves make a contribution to efficiency and productivity. And here it has been argued forcefully that the institutional loyalty that is in this way gained precisely pays such dividends. The analogy with IHEs is clear. See Reichheld, 1996, chapters 4 and 5.

The second comment pertains to those nonregular faculty members who are teaching full time. One might have clever debates about just what constitutes such a full-time job, but in the end it comes down to the hours a competent, conscientious person is at work—in class, conferring with students, preparing for class, grading tests and papers. When those hours add up to eight and more, when it becomes less and less plausible that someone could, in an ongoing way, take on additional work, that measure has been reached. And when that happens, the compensation must be high enough to amount to a living wage—modest, perhaps, but sufficient for a reasonable living, as that is measured by salaries elsewhere in the community.

A reply might be made that even when full time, these nonregular faculty positions are only temporary and should thus not be compared with normal jobs that one has and keeps to earn one's livelihood. Such a response stands a strong chance of being sophistical. In many cases, these nonregular jobs are temporary solely because the institution will commit itself only for a year at a time. Temporary by fiat, in other words, and often merely *de jure*, since many people are appointed to do the same work year after year after year. Many of these full-time positions are in fact not temporary and are held by people who live on what they earn. Thus, the classification of these positions as temporary is a legalism that does not itself justify reduced compensation.

There is thus a further point to be made, in addition to the matter of paying a living wage. IHEs have an obligation to make the lives of many of their nonregular faculty more predictable and secure. Since institutions can foresee many of their needs, at least for a few years, and are thus able to provide greater security for a sizeable fraction of their nonregular faculty by issuing multiyear contracts, they ought to do so. In several ways, to sum up, many nonregular faculty members are treated inequitably by the institutions that engage them. And it is precisely because they are variously exploited that their employment is economically so advantageous that their numbers have become so large. Accordingly, were one to follow more closely the dictates of morality, the economic benefits would decrease and this cadre would undoubtedly shrink. This would leave IHEs with a healthier mix of regular and nonregular faculty.

II. Some Moral Aspects of the Tenure Decision

The decision to confer indefinite tenure on a faculty member still on probation—or to withhold it—is a good sample of a personnel decision to look at, both because it is peculiar to IHEs and because it tends to be the result of a most elaborate process.[5] But precisely because of that complexity, it is worthwhile to isolate some of the ethical principles that bear even on personnel decisions in much simpler contexts. We begin, therefore, by imagining a small enterprise, such as a neighborhood supermarket, with just four levels of employees: workers without supervisory roles, department heads, assistant managers, and the manager. And we will try to state some of the moral principles that are relevant when an assistant manager's position opens and one or several department heads (and no outsiders) are considered for promotion to that position.

The obvious requirements are the obligation to be fair to each candidate and to treat each of them as a person. But when the promotions process is looked at under a magnifying glass, this broad injunction can be seen to be composed of several components.

(1) *Equal treatment.* Fairness requires that all candidates for promotion be treated in the same way, from informing eligible candidates, to gathering evidence, to the manner of consideration. Fairness prohibits playing favorites.

All department heads need to be informed (and only they, assuming that this position is a requirement); each must be instructed regarding the procedure for applying; and the method by which candidates are considered—perusal of written material, consultation of referees, interview—must be similar for everyone.

(2) *The evidence considered must be relevant and complete.* Every person has an indefinitely large number of characteristics and abilities. For the performance of any given job, only a subclass of these is brought into play. Fairness requires that all and only the (available) evidence for the presence (or absence) of traits that are relevant becomes an ingredient in the decision.

The manager must not weigh irrelevant characteristics in the decision—neither be "prejudiced" against a race or hair color, nor prefer someone from the same neighborhood—that is, the employer must not pay heed to any trait that plays no role in the performance of the envisaged duties. Evidence that the candidate nags her husband is irrelevant if there is no evidence that she nags her co-workers.

(3) *Conscientiousness of consideration.* Since evidence can be considered cursorily or thoroughly, one needs to point out that fairness calls for being conscientious in carrying out that task.

Thoroughness is most likely limited to interviewing several supervisors who are acquainted with a candidate's performance, interviewing the candidate, and examining evidence (tests, work samples) concerning the ability to perform skilled tasks, such as doing accounting. To give inadequate consideration is to jump to conclusions without making use of an appropriate quantity of evidence.

(4) *Timeliness of the decision.* Just as morality requires that justice be swift, so there is an obligation to candidates for promotion to know of the decision in a timely manner, both for the sake of mental comfort and to permit candidates to plan their lives.

(5) *Candor.* Concern for the candidate as a person—with a life to lead and plans to make—requires that when a promotion is not granted, and when the candidate desires it, he or she be provided with the reasons for this failure. The power to decide implies the obligation to be candid.

(6) *Promulgation of conditions for promotion.* The process by means of which it is decided whether someone is or is not promoted cannot be fair unless the candidate knows all relevant aspects of this process. Three components seem crucial.

(a) Potential candidates need to know whether promotion of a given sort is possible. Promotion must not be like grace that is granted to whom it is granted, even if the grantor has good reasons. This calls for the promulgation of a policy that clearly sets forth who is eligible for consideration for promotion to which posts.

(b) Potential candidates need to know what is desired in a successful candidate for promotion and what is considered to be evidence for the possession of the desired characteristics. Here it must be conveyed with sufficient clarity—however informally—what skills and experience are needed to be appointed assistant manager and what kind of references, tests, and interviews are considered relevant evidence.

(c) Potential candidates must be apprised as to how they should proceed to apply for promotion, so that they can act to be considered.

When one turns to the tenure decision, one is immediately struck by the multiplicity of levels that are involved. Departmental committees recommend to departments and departmental chairpersons; these, in turn, recommend to the dean. Further, at some institutions a committee specifically formed to advise on a particular case so recommends, while at others a standing committee on promotion and tenure performs that task; both function at still others. The dean, in turn, recommends to the chief academic officer—who may or may not also seek the advice of a committee—who, in turn, recommends to the president, who recommends to a board of trustees.

The reading of such a summary induces sympathy with the nonacademic's puzzlement about our cumbersome processes. But what perplexes outsiders also becomes fertile soil for the mistreatment of those about whom decisions are made. At worst, the process that leads to a tenure decision resembles the trial of Josef K. or an impenetrable black box issuing verdicts. Even when a procedure actually *is* fair, murkiness of process combined with the length of time it takes to get done are sources of anxiety to the candidate. To the degree to which unclarity and delays are unnecessary, they are immoral. At the same time, it must be conceded that at least one cause of anxiety can't be eliminated. For good decision making in a setting in which criteria are complex and collegiality is a central value requires both a complex process and long stretch of time from its beginning to a conclusion. The task, accordingly, is to maximize clarity of role and accountability, measures that will contribute both to the adequacy of the decisions made and to the confidence the community will have that the process is fair.

What must be clear, above all, is the locus of the decision itself. The manager of the supermarket decides who will be assistant manager. Who decides whether someone attains tenure or not? For the process to be morally acceptable, the functions of the numerous participants must be specified: some *advise*, others *recommend,* and one person must be identified as the *maker of the decision*. That academic administrator—the dean, the academic vice president, or the president, depending on the institution—must thus regard as *advisors* all those who contributed, directly or indirectly, to the recommendation now on his or her desk and must look upon himself or herself as the person who decides, even if by custom a recommendation constitutes a severe constraint. Moreover, the fact that in virtually all IHEs there are "higher" powers who have the right to overturn the decision made "lower" down should not be permitted to confuse the point just made. There is a normal decision maker—the dean, for example—who has certain duties (yet to be discussed) if the process is to be ethically acceptable. Nothing is changed by the fact that provost, president, or board of trustees might overrule and that sometimes they do. It merely follows that when (and only when) a higher authority actually *does* overrule, a limited number of duties normally assigned to the normal decision maker—such as providing reasons for a negative decision to the candidate—are transferred to the person who made the final decision.

The clear identification of a normal decision maker—here, for convenience, called the dean—is a necessary condition for adequate treatment of at least four ethical issues central to this promotion process.

(1) As decision maker, the dean is in charge of the entire process, with ultimate responsibility for the designation of the participants and the assignment and performance of their roles. This is the case even where faculty legislation "dictates" much of the procedure. Where a governance scheme does not support responsibility with authority, it must thus be seen as morally flawed.

(2) The dean, in our hypothesis, is responsible for the articulation of

the criteria that function in the decision about promotion to tenure. However complex the collegial process that formulates them in the first place, they "become" those of the person applying them in a decision.

(3) The person who makes the decision is the person who must conscientiously weigh the evidence. This requirement is intimately tied to the management of the process that amasses the evidence in the first place. But it also implies that the dean cannot hide behind such a process and blame its inadequacy for the inadequacy with which the evidence might have been collected or consulted.

(4) The dean, like the manager of the supermarket, is the person who must give the reasons to a candidate for a failure to promote, should the reasons be requested. In this way, a candidate would be provided with a means for partially assessing the fairness of the judgment and be helped in assessing his or her future prospects in the profession.

The decision process is complex, we have said, because both academic administrators and different faculty units participate in it. But it is also complex because the criterion—or, if one prefers, the plurality of interrelated criteria—is complex as well: the canonical trio, teaching, research, and service, are neither incommensurable nor individually quantifiable in any satisfactory way. Each component is manifested differently in different fields, and, even within a field, satisfactoriness and excellence have many different guises. Moreover, for many reasons, these criteria (and not just the stringency of standards) vary from institution to institution.

Nevertheless, in spite of this complicatedness, there is an obligation to promulgate. Broad statements can be made to the faculty community, and such statements can convey useful information, even if their precision is limited. What evidence about teaching is considered, and how much? Does advising matter, or supervising doctoral candidates? Is community service a serious ingredient, and, if so, within what limitations? Do the products of research need to be published in refereed publications? A fair personnel process requires conveying to potential candidates what is called for from faculty members who would be tenured. Still, we should acknowledge that we cannot actually spell out criteria of acceptability (including a threshold degree of excellence) in a long disjunction; we must rely instead on making comparisons, tacit and explicit, with relevant exemplary individuals who are recognized as deserving their tenured status and with the accomplishments that brought them there. And this ultimate "ineffability" of the criterion of promotability makes it most susceptible to distortion and thus puts the burden of fairness squarely on the participants in the process and on how they do their jobs.

Before returning to a discussion of the process, some brief comments on one desideratum for promotability that is particularly vulnerable to distortion. Since tenure constitutes a contract of indefinite term, how the candidate can be expected to "fit in" is a question that is inevitably asked, even if not always explicitly. However professional one's attitude, such considerations cannot be altogether purged from the criterion of acceptability. What if the would-be tenured colleague is a congenital liar and never reliable *as* a colleague? What if he or she is subject to frequent uncontrolled temper tantrums that disrupt all meetings and all such common tasks as creating a collective final examination? If, then, we must pay some attention to the capacity to pitch in, to work with others, to cooperate in a common enterprise, there is also a real danger of sliding from reasonable concern to the unethical use of irrelevant information.* Thus, there is prejudice against women, as well as against people who tend to be grubby; there is animosity toward blacks, and there is aversion to fat people. The moral obligation of those who decide on tenure is to consider for the formulation of a judgment only those characteristics that play a role in the performance of relevant functions. Accordingly, where failure to fit in is not dependent on predicted behavior of the candidate, but simply on the views and feelings of the group, morality rules it out from consideration.

As we now return to the procedure employed in making decisions about tenure, I want to single out three issues. First, some observations about the selection and organization of the individuals who will participate in the decision. To begin with, institutions vary greatly in the number and kinds of faculty levels that play a role in a tenure decision, and by no means do all such differences have ethical implications. But it very much does matter that there be more than one faculty level, with the "higher" representing a broader constituency than the "lower." In this way a wider perspective is introduced, capable of serving as a potential check to parochialism, a limitation that tends to give too much prominence to personal traits of marginal relevance.

It also matters that the method of selecting participants be the same for each class of candidates. Arbitrariness in the designation of those who help make judgments is an enemy of fairness. Moreover, those who are selected to stand in judgment of the candidate must be appropriate for that role. That faculty members of the same or lower rank should not be party to the formulation of a recommendation is widely understood. Actual or potential competitors cannot seem to be fair

---

*The academy must be more tolerant of eccentricity than most institutions; it must have room for the "mad genius" where society stands to benefit from the work of that genius, even though the madness exacts a price. At the same time, it has to be admitted that institutions vary in the degree to which they can afford to tolerate certain eccentricities. In tight places, most everyone is needed to pitch in; in plusher institutions, there is more give.

judges, even if in fact they are capable of the requisite objectivity. There is, by way of interesting contrast, more disagreement about the role students should play, with both extremes—full participation and no role at all—finding passionate defenders. The introduction of a criterion and of a distinction will be helpful in sorting out this controversy.

Those who appropriately participate in the recommendation of a promotion should surely be qualified to do so, and we have no choice but to assume that credentialed colleagues are qualified. Students, on the other hand, lack those credentials. They are generally unable to judge a faculty member's research and service, if only because they have not acquired the experience of dealing knowledgeably with testimony and letters of reference on such topics. Even if one assumes, then, that students are capable of determining the effectiveness of a faculty member as a teacher, the handicaps just mentioned would make them very unequal participants in the formulation of a judgment to be based on so much broader a criterion. But students do have a perspective—derived from knowledge and from concern—that is not possessed by faculty colleagues in equal measure. As the institution's leading clients, their perspective is relevant to providing a full account of the work of a faculty member. And the tension between these two observations is best reconciled by means of the distinction between participant and consultant. Just as departmental and other committees consult scholars throughout the world about the quality and importance of a candidate's research (without having those scholars participate in the formulation of a summary judgment), so the faculty can turn to student committees and to records of the evaluation of teaching by students to obtain advice from this constituency of the academy.

But there is an additional aspect to being qualified which, though of considerable ethical relevance, is nonetheless often ignored. Credentials are a necessary but not a sufficient qualifying condition for taking part in deciding. Justified participation must be informed participation; no voice should be permitted to speak, unless its owner has done the homework that entitles having a voice. To participate in deciding without having a grasp of the material about a candidate that was systematically collected to serve as the basis of the required judgment introduces an element of arbitrariness at best and irrelevant prejudice—for or against—at worst. Administrators of the promotions process have a duty to ensure that participants are qualified by being prepared.

Third, fairness (not to mention good decision making) requires that each group that functions in the recommending process engage in face-to-face discussions on the issue of the merit of the candidate. Members of departmental committees, departmental senior faculties, ad hoc committees, promotions committees—whatever the units—must not simply be polled for a count of votes; rather, their members must have been present during informed discussions of all aspects of the case. Absence must imply disenfranchisement and a reduction, at best, to the role of (nonvoting) consultant.

Two reasons support this thesis. One follows from the complexity of the criteria of tenurability: multifaceted, incommensurable, nonquantifiable. It is complicated in exactly the way that calls for the deployment of more than one mind, if all aspects are to be adequately seen and weighed. There is here a reasonable expectation that the picture of a candidate that emerges at the end of a discussion will have greater verisimilitude than any that might earlier have been produced by one participant alone. Yet still more important than this positive result is the efficacy of discussion for dispelling misapprehensions and jumping to conclusions of all kinds. The clash of opinions in discussion tends to combat error and unwarranted assumptions. No one *eligible* to vote on the fate of a candidate (and of the institution) should therefore have the *right* to vote without having participated in a discussion with informed peers.

Unethical behavior is possible in broad daylight, but no doubt the risk of its occurrence becomes greater under the cover of confidentiality. Mostly we know when we do something wrong; having other people in a position to find out has a tendency to discourage us—at least in such polite circles as the academy. Prima facie, an ethical case can be made against the practice of confidentiality in personnel decisions: an open process is more likely to be fair to the candidate being considered. Moreover, the lifting of confidentiality would certainly eliminate much of the anxiety that is engendered by the opaqueness of the decision process.

But clearly more is to be said if one reflects on some of the reasons for the practice of confidentiality. Leave aside the important (and ethically relevant) consideration of protecting candidates from public exposure—from a display of their actual inadequacies to expressions of half-truths, surmises, and occasional lies about them. Surely, confidentiality is practiced because it is believed that if assured of privacy, participants will make "more honest" (here meaning "harsher") assessments of candidates and will in this way better serve the institution.

I have no doubt that this is so. The academic world is not a tough world, populated by strong egos ready to "mix it up" in personal slugging matches. Further, collegial participation is in good part voluntary and often constitutes an unwelcome intrusion on the central activities of the teacher/scholar. Certainly the referee who gives time to a sister institution by making and conveying judgments about the work of a candidate does so as a volunteer, often a reluctant one. Given these underlying truths, it is highly likely (though subject to empirical testing) that decisions made by means of a process that eschews confidentiality will be "softer" and lean somewhat more toward the candidate and away from the standards of the institution.

But the point to be made about this observation, assuming it to be true, is that such leaning away from the interests of the institution is not ethically neutral; it cannot be granted that the field of morality belongs entirely to candidates, so that anything that might improve their chances of success constitutes moral improvement. That institution, after all, is made up of present and future students and faculty colleagues and, in a world of finite resources, on future candidates for the same status. If, thus, confidentiality improves the process's fairness to the *institution*, that too has ethical relevance. In any case, several of the measures earlier stressed will act to reduce the likelihood of negative ethical consequences of confidentiality. A nonarbitrary way of selecting the participants in a process, including the thoughtful designation of scholar/consultants on the candidate's work, becomes important. So is discussion at all levels, where distortions stand a chance of being revealed and countered. Crucial, finally, is the assumption of responsibility by the academic administrator who is the decision maker for the integrity of the process as a whole.*

One final observation. Like all institutions, IHEs have a way of veiling the fact that individuals are moral agents by permitting academic administrators and faculty alike to hide behind rules and procedures that were formulated by anonymous earlier administrators or legislated by faculties acting corporately. But in the end, *individuals* decide, *individuals* act, and the fate of *individuals* is determined by personnel decisions, including present and future students, present and future colleagues. Since to academic administrators and to faculty members significant roles in the personnel processes of the academy are assigned, they bear a responsibility both for the ethical acceptability of the procedures used and for the way in which they are implemented from case to case.

Notes

1. See chapter 4, section II.
2. See chapter 5, section III.

---

*The practice of confidentiality is under legal and legislative pressure from a variety of sides. It is not inconceivable that in a decade or so, it will, for all practical purposes, have disappeared from personnel decisions in the academy. My optimistic speculation has it that after a dip in the quality of decision making, the academy will slowly make a transition to adulthood and its citizens will learn to accept public scrutiny of tough decisions.

3. Literally the day after these paragraphs were first drafted, an article appeared in *The New York Times*, starting on the front page, with the headline "Scholars Fear 'Star' System May Undercut Their Mission." It says almost everything that is being said here and names names to boot. See Janny Scott, 1997, A1 and, though without names, Appendix 6, below.

4. See chapter 5, section II.

5. What follows is an abridgment and slight modification of Weingartner, 1990.

Postscript

Most everything that is asserted in this book under the general heading of "moral dimensions of academic administration" is predicated on the claim that IHEs are *professional* institutions that serve a number of categories of clients, above all the students studying there and a broader society that benefits from the intellectual creativity of the academy. What has been maintained rests, furthermore, on the claim that the most important members of colleges and universities—namely their faculties, which carry out the bulk of the primary functions of their institutions—are themselves professionals, with quite complex relationships to their activities and their places of work.

If these central theses of professionalism were denied, it is not at all clear that there is such a topic as the moral dimensions of specifically academic administration. What there would be to discuss are ethical issues pertaining to an administering and managing that would be difficult to distinguish from what is to be found in the literature on business ethics. One would write about applications of principles of fairness, moral and immoral uses of power, and much more. But while all of these themes would have their own particular forms because they have their lives in academic institutions, so are they manifested differently when one looks at the management of a steel mill, a firm producing software, or a worldwide travel agency. But insofar as these latter industries don't warrant separate volumes about the moral dimensions of management there, there would not be much warrant to include a book on administration in this series.

But that the special character of academic institutions should be denied is not just hypothetical supposing, for it has been and is under attack from several quarters. It will be worthwhile to consider briefly the sources of these assaults and to sketch out how they do or would undermine the character of IHEs as it has here been understood—and therefore the moral dimensions of academic administration.

119

(1) Take, first, *consumerism on the part of students* and compliance with that view on the part of the academic institution. Students, on this assumption, are customers with certain interests and desires, and the college or university is the vendor whose job it is to provide what they want. In the late sixties, the cry was relevance and student choice. In many an institution, students succeeded in having most or all requirements eliminated and numerous individual courses, especially in the humanities and the social sciences, focus on contemporary and popular material. It was in those days that Shakespeare gave way to the detective story as the subject matter of well attended literature courses. It was in those days that I saw in the bookstore at Vassar (where I was then teaching) B. F. Skinner's *Walden II* piled for use in a dozen courses each semester.

But in many ways, those were the days of the higher consumerism. The motivation, if in many ways misguided, was intellectual: students wanted to know what they thought was relevant to their lives. The consumerism of the nineties is of the plain vanilla kind. Students conceive of themselves as paying for certain goods and insist in various ways—many of them quite coercive—on getting them. (The fact is, of course, that seldom do the students pay, but their parents, who may thus also act as consumers, ignoring that tuition is usually supplemented by financial contributions on the part of the IHE—either directly, in the form of scholarships or because even full tuition doesn't pay in full for the educative and other activities performed for its students—and ignoring that, for many institutions, the taxpayers are the primary supporters.) And the goods that student consumers desire in the nineties, to put things bluntly, are not so much an education of a certain kind, but records and degrees they regard as needed to make their ways in the world.[1]

To the extent to which the administration of a college or university "merely" ignores such student consumerism, it exposes a significant portion of its faculty—the untenured, above all—to pressures that have them compromise their professional judgment regarding course content and grading in response to the need to satisfy their students. To the extent to which administrations acquiesce or collaborate with their "customers," as many did in the sixties, they come to direct faculties to act in ways that short-circuit their professional role. ("An Ivy League professor said recently that if tenure disappeared, universities would be 'free to sell diplomas outright.' "[2]) Administrators would be the people to determine what is wanted and to manage their faculties in ways that assured that those goods were delivered. One might here insert a lament regarding the faculty's loss of academic freedom. But, in our context at least, it would seem to be even more fundamental that such administrative collusion with student consumers comes close to converting what was a professional institution into a provider of services for which there happens to be a market, on the order of barber shops or travel agencies.

(2) Everything that was said about institutional collaboration with student consumerism is heightened to the maximum degree where a college or university exists *to make a profit.* Indeed, the "logic" of student consumerism points to profit making; for why should an institution not reap a benefit if it supplies wares for which purchasers exist? The notion of professional service to a *client* is replaced by the conception of a *vendor* of products that are wanted in the *marketplace.* Such an institution will be profitable to the degree to which its administration can determine what the market wants and maintain a faculty that works to satisfy those demands, both with respect to course content and the evaluation of students. Administrators become full-time managers of employees who perform desired services, and faculty members become the employees who serve.

It will not be otherwise. While individuals in business to make a profit may (heroically) be capable of setting sharp limits as to what they are willing to do, of all the practices that are legal in their lines of work, it is highly improbable that a large and complex institution would have the same capacity, not to mention actually use it. If an establishment's goal is profit, all of its activities and all of its personnel are evaluated for the contributions they make toward bringing in that profit. To survive as a member of the enterprise, not to mention to thrive in it, requires success in that regard, whether, in this case, what is or is not done is educationally sound. Would-be academic administrators become department managers in a commercial enterprise.*

(3) Trends exist that, if extended, would convert certain institutions funded by states or municipalities into what one might call *public utili-*

---

*"The consumer appetite for less rigorous education is nowhere more evident than in the University of Phoenix, a profit-making school that shuns traditional scholarship and offers a curriculum so superficial that critics compare it to a drive-through restaurant . . . , a university [that] has expanded to 60 sites around the country, and more than 40,000 students, making it the country's largest private university" (Staples, 1998). That makes the word "university" a homonym, with a quite different meaning when placed before "of Pennsylvania" or in front of "of Phoenix." A similar "deprofessionalization" is taking place in for-profit health maintenance organizations (HMOs), largely by taking away from physicians the power to make medical decisions regarding their patients. To cite one example from a hair-raising article, a memo from the HMO United Behavioral Systems "to its nine mental-health clinics in the Minneapolis-St. Paul area explains that the case of any patient needing more than eight sessions will be referred to a supervisory panel . . . [whose] principal question should be: 'What needs to happen in order to terminate the patient?' " (Finkelstein, 1996, 26).

ties. There are cases of a shifting of the authority of faculties and administrative leadership to determine the content of students' education to governmental agencies, supervisory boards, and even legislators. This intervention can take the form of having courses and programs that are mandated, or it can take the form of "assessment" that measures and insists upon certain "student outcomes." When this current jargon is translated into ordinary English, we see that a governmental agency can have a powerful effect on what is taught by requiring that students be tested for the possession of certain knowledge and skills and requiring them to perform satisfactorily if they are to graduate. One impetus in this direction might be called governmental or taxpayer consumerism: If taxes are going to pay for these expensive institutions, those who provide the money are entitled to determine what is done with it. Additional motivation no doubt comes from the current ascendancy of anti-intellectualism in this country (where intellectuals tend to be thought of as liberal and godless) that wants to curb the autonomy of IHEs.

While it may not be too far off the mark to refer to some of the community colleges as public utilities, I know of no instances of four-year colleges or universities in which this transfer of authority has gone particularly far. The trend, however, is there, and one can imagine pressures on the American social fabric that would accelerate such developments. And while public institutions are above all vulnerable to the forces that bring changes of this kind, even private institutions are not in principle immune to them. In the scheme De George uses to classify types of universities, the processes here pointed to have the tendency to transform the "traditional model"—which has been the subject of this book—in the direction of the "ideological model."[3] For, after all, "ideology" need not take the relatively global and monolithic form that it had in the heyday of the former Soviet Union, the universities of which are the originals of this model. A much more homespun ideology, diffuse and local, can also be corrosive and convert faculty into executors of the wishes of the state and academic administrators into the managers who are retained to make sure that what is wanted happens.

(4) In a period in which the success of the American private enterprise economy has made it the model for the whole world to emulate, some boards of trustees of private IHEs, and even public ones, have eagerly talked of imposing the *corporate model* on the academic institutions they oversee. These (mostly) men of the world regard their academic institution's president as its chief executive officer and most lesser academic administrators as vice presidents of different grades. Their notion, often, is that these administrators should, without so much fuss and bother, get the job done sans profuse faculty palaver, not to say without faculty obstructionism, as it looks to them. They pine for the ef-

ficiency that is induced by an ever-present need to be concerned about the bottom line.

No doubt many IHEs could benefit from greater efficiency in how they go about their business. The pervasiveness, for example, of a certain kind of caution and hesitancy on the part of administrators to make decisions without elaborate committee "protection"—even when the institution's rules permit it—can be costly in time and, therefore, money. But improvement in matters such as these would not be taken to be much more than tinkering at the edges. Desirable, to be sure, but woefully inadequate as a replication of how an American corporation works. But, then, just what would do that? How can the wisdom that board members acquired in the business world be applied to the college or university whose guardians they are?

In order truly to rethink the role of academic administrators as corporate executives and managers, on the one hand, and faculty members as their employees, on the other, they must find some IHE equivalent to a product, on the one hand, and a quantifiable bottom line, on the other. Strictly speaking, of course, that is not possible; in particular, success cannot be measured in profit actually brought in. But striving toward quantifiable goals is not ruled out: one can aim to increase the enrollment, for example, to raise larger amounts of money from donors and alumni, to bring in more dollars to support research from various governmental agencies—and the like.

It is worth pointing out, to begin with, that to the extent to which the business world is in this way mimicked, the effect is reductionist. More students are enrolled; but what are the characteristics of those students—their abilities, their programmatic interests, their social, ethnic, geographical profiles? More money is raised; but for what purposes are these funds designated, and how are those purposes related to the goals of the institution? Increased research support is brought in; but for what kinds of projects, and how are they and the faculty that undertakes them related to a broader institutional mission, and how are they to be assessed as contributions to society? Such questions can of course be answered. But as soon as the answers are considered and evaluated, the cherished simplicity and quantifiability disappears.

But the push to impose the corporate model requires making sure that the performance of administrators remains measurable, since accountability is thought to depend on that fact. When the push is hard enough and, to a degree, successful, the result is a hierarchical organization, rather than a collaborative one, with administrators directing the faculty. Certain things must be done in order to bring in more students and to keep them enrolled: The judgment of the educator must largely yield to that of the vendor. The president and the development department raise more money: faculty and staff then engage in those activities for which that money has come in, thus shaping the institution. Bringing in more research dollars is rewarded: The question as to what are the most valuable research projects to undertake is replaced by the question as to what projects will bring in the largest number of dollars.

One can see how pressures such as these are likely to change the entire culture of academic institutions; our concern here, however, is limited to their effects on the nature of administration. And there are no surprises in that domain. To the extent to which the corporate model is adopted by an IHE, its administrators become managers analogous to the executives of a business corporation. There is no reason, then, why the ethical issues that are raised for them will not be more or less adequately dealt with in the pages of a book on business ethics.

(5) The *unionizing of the faculty* of an academic institution is the last way to be taken up here in which the special professionalism of academic institutions and their leading members is undermined. Although such a move may well be undertaken in reaction to policies and activities of agencies, boards of directors, or administrators, it is an action taken by the faculty itself, not infrequently at the cost of great effort and bitterness. In one analysis, unionization in higher education is a product of the conflict between two competing principles to be found within any academic institution, the professional model and the bureaucratic system.[4] Because the faculty professionals are also salaried employees, the power is with the bureaucracy, of which administrators are the chief representatives. Faculty unions are formed in the effort to redress some of that imbalance of power and to secure better compensation and working conditions.

I want to claim that it is precisely a chief obligation of academic administrators to bridge the gap between these two realms or, rather, to do their work in such a way that the professional character of an IHE dominates the bureaucratic principle, though it must be admitted that there are no doubt situations where that is exceedingly difficult to bring off. In any case, the warning of a frequently cited passage about the creation of faculty unions and ensuing collective bargaining was well taken: "In dividing the university into worker-professors and manager-administrators and governing boards, it imperils the premise of shared authority, encourages the polarization in interests, and exaggerates the adversary concerns over interests held in common."[5]

Above all, given the specific concerns of this book, the distinction between academic administration and management in the business world tends to disappear.[6] Because collective bargaining not only discourages individual bargaining, but tends strongly to favor such "objective" criteria as seniority over "subjective" judgments of merit, the management of salaries in a college or university will come to resemble that task in a factory. Further, when professors think of themselves as workers, the concept of tenure ultimately reduces to that of job security, regarded as "the *right* of all qualified and competent faculty and professional staff"[7] to be awarded to any who has performed competently during a relatively short probationary period.

These two effects are significant symbols of the fact that "the principles that evolved over many generations in 'blue-collar unionism' have been successfully transferred to academe in spite of the enormous differences in structure and role."[8] But a further result brings home the fact that the formation of a faculty union is likely to undermine the premises needed for there to *be* moral issues concerning specifically *academic* administration, because it tends to undermine the collaboration in which faculty and administration jointly steer the institution toward the accomplishment of its goals. "[T]he very existence of union representation must serve to reduce interest in and participation in faculty senates, councils, or other bodies. The adversary model of university governance . . . , with consequent spelling out of both rights and obligations— e.g. student contact hours, research time, faculty-student ratios—is likely to weaken the 'producers' cooperative,' self-government aspects."[9] The bargaining unit and management negotiate, just as they do in a textile mill.

Some of the trends here sketched out are more with us than others, but none of them is mere alarmist fiction. Moreover, wherever any of these tendencies is actualized in a college or university beyond a certain threshold, the very topic of this book becomes moot: Academic administration becomes management so that its moral dimensions are covered in discussions of business ethics. That fact, while of local interest for this book, would of course only be a symptom that is overshadowed by a much larger and more fundamental reality. If the trends taken up in this postscript were to become widespread they would bring about the demise of traditional colleges and universities—institutions that, in spite of all of their flaws, have performed invaluable services for this country and society more generally. Their successor institutions would, of course, perform many needed functions; life would go on. It is difficult to believe, however, that without essentially autonomous colleges and universities that are engaged in teaching, undertaking research and scholarship, and subjecting the policies and assumptions of the day to criticism, we would be living in a world that is truly civilized.

Notes

1. See, for example, Staples, 1998.
2. Staples, 1998.

3. See De George, 1997, 10–11.

4. Lewis and Ryan, 1977, 143–46.

5. Kadish, 1972, 122; also see, below, Appendix 7, 167.

6. What follows leans on the careful study, Ladd and Lipset, 1973, chapter 6, "Effects of Unionism on Higher Education," 69–95. Extensive personal observation suggests that, with respect to this topic, not much has changed in the twenty-five years since the study's publication.

7. An AFT position paper quoted in Ladd and Lipset, 1973, 72; italics added.

8. Ladd and Lipset, 1973, 81.

9. Ladd and Lipset, 1973, 85; but see the entire section on the effect of unionization on governance, 81–88.

Appendix 1

Educational Institutions as Tax Exempt

Section 501(c)(3) of the Internal Revenue Code provides that an organization may be exempt from federal income tax if it is organized and operated exclusively for an "educational" purpose. The term "educational" is a broad term and thus many educational organizations are also charitable in nature, as the term "charitable" includes the "advancement of education."

Scope of Term "Educational"

The federal government has adopted a definition of the term "educational" as encompassing far more than formal schooling. Basically, the concept of "educational" as used for federal tax purposes is defined as relating to the "instruction or training of the individual for the purpose of improving or developing his capabilities" or the "instruction of the public on subjects useful to the individual and beneficial to the community."

For many years, the definition accorded the term "educational" by the Department of the Treasury and the IRS was routinely followed. However, in 1980, a federal court of appeals found portions of the regulation defining the term unconstitutionally vague. In a 1983 opinion, this appellate court—albeit recognizing "the inherently general nature of the term 'educational' and the wide range of meanings Congress may have intended to convey," and stating that "[w]e do not attempt a definition" of the term—set forth some general criteria as to what material may qualify as "educational."

Bruce R. Hopkins. *The Law of Tax-Exempt Organizations*. Sixth edition. New York: John Wiley & Sons, 1992. From chapter 8, "Educational Organizations," 177–78, 183–85. References have been omitted. Copyright © 1992, John Wiley & Sons. Reprinted by permission of John Wiley & Sons, Inc.

In the subsequent case, this federal appellate court decided that the materials there at issue "fall short" of being educational, "[e]ven under the most minimal requirement of a rational development of a point of view." Said the court: "It is the fact that there is no reasoned development of the conclusions which removes it [the material at issue] from any definition of 'educational' conceivably intended by Congress." Moreover, the court ruled, "in order to be deemed 'educational' and enjoy tax exemption some degree of intellectually appealing development of or foundation for the views advocated would be required." The court wrote:

> The exposition of propositions the correctness of which is readily demonstrable is doubtless educational. As the truth of the view asserted becomes less and less demonstrable, however, "instruction" or "education" must, we think, require more than mere assertion and repetition.

Thereafter, the court observed that, "[i]n attempting a definition suitable for all comers, IRS, or any legislature, court, or other administrator is beset with difficulties which are obvious."

Formal Educational Organizations

Nonprofit educational institutions, such as primary, secondary, and postsecondary schools, colleges and universities, early childhood centers, and trade schools, are "educational" organizations for federal tax law purposes. These organizations all have, as required, "a regularly scheduled curriculum, a regular faculty, and a regularly enrolled body of students in attendance at the place where the educational activities are regularly carried on." To be tax-exempt, however, the schools must, like all "charitable" organizations, meet all of the tax law requirements pertaining to these entities, including a showing that they are operated for public, rather than private, interests.

• • •

Instruction of the Public

As noted, the income tax regulations state that the term "educational" as used for federal tax purposes relates, in part, to the "instruction of the public on subjects useful to the individual and beneficial to the community." In many instances, an organization is considered "educational," both because it is regarded as instructing the public as well as the individual. Nevertheless, even though it is difficult (and probably unnecessary) to formulate rigid distinctions between the two types of educational purposes, three categories of the former purpose have emerged.

One category of this type of educational organization is the one that provides certain "personal services" deemed beneficial to the general public. The IRS, under this rationale, has ruled to be tax-exempt an organization that provided marriage counseling services, that disseminated information concerning hallucinatory drugs, that conducted personal money management instruction, that educated expectant mothers and the public in a method of painless childbirth, that counseled women on methods of resolving unwanted pregnancies, that counseled widows and widowers to assist them in legal, financial, and emotional problems caused by the deaths of their spouses, and that counseled men concerning methods of voluntary sterilization. Similarly, an organization that functioned primarily as a crop seed certification entity was held to be educational because of its adult education classes, seminars, newsletter, and lending library.

Another category of educational organizations is those that endeavor to instruct the public in the field of civic betterment. In this regard, this type of organization frequently also qualifies under one or more varieties of the concept of "charitable" or "social welfare." Thus, an organization that disseminated information, in the nature of results of its investigations, in an effort to lessen racial and religious prejudice in the fields of housing and public accommodations was ruled to be tax-exempt. Other organizations in this category include ones that distributed information about the results of a model demonstration housing program for low-income families conducted by it, disseminated information on the need for international cooperation, educated the public as to the means of correcting conditions such as community tension and juvenile delinquency, enlightened the public in a particular city as to the advantages of street planning, developed and distributed a community land-use plan, and educated the public regarding environmental deterioration due to solid waste pollution, radio and television programming, and accuracy of news coverage by newspapers.

The third category of educational organizations that exist to instruct the public is those that conduct study and research. The variety of efforts encompassed by these organizations is nearly limitless. As illustrations, these organizations include those that conducted analyses, studies, and research into the problems of a particular region (pollution, transportation, water resources, waste disposal) and published the results, and published a journal to disseminate information about specific types of physical and mental disorders.

Appendix 2

Statement on Professional Ethics of the American Association of University Professors

*The statement which follows, a revision of a statement origi-
nally adopted in 1966, was approved by the Association's
Committee B on Professional Ethics, adopted by the Association's Council in June 1987, and endorsed by the Seventy-
third Annual Meeting.*

Introduction

From its inception, the American Association of University Professors
has recognized that membership in the academic profession carries with
it special responsibilities. The Association has consistently affirmed
these responsibilities in major policy statements, providing guidance to
professors in such matters as their utterances as citizens, the exercise of
their responsibilities to students and colleagues, and their conduct when
resigning from an institution or when undertaking sponsored research.
The *Statement on Professional Ethics* that follows sets forth those general standards that serve as a reminder of the variety of responsibilities
assumed by all members of the profession.

In the enforcement of ethical standards, the academic profession differs from those of law and medicine, whose associations act to ensure
the integrity of members engaged in private practice. In the academic
profession the individual institution of higher learning provides this assurance and so should normally handle questions concerning propriety
of conduct within its own framework by reference to a faculty group.

American Association of University Professors. *Policy Documents & Reports*. Washington, D.C.: AAUP, 105–106. Reprinted by permission of the
AAUP.

The Association supports such local action and stands ready, through the general secretary and Committee B, to counsel with members of the academic community concerning questions of professional ethics and to inquire into complaints when local consideration is impossible or inappropriate. If the alleged offense is deemed sufficiently serious to raise the possibility of adverse action, the procedures should be in accordance with the 1940 *Statement of Principles on Academic Freedom and Tenure,* the 1958 *Statement on Procedural Standards in Faculty Dismissal Proceedings,* or the applicable provisions of the Association's *Recommended Institutional Regulations on Academic Freedom and Tenure.*

The Statement

I. Professors, guided by a deep conviction of the worth and dignity of the advancement of knowledge, recognize the special responsibilities placed upon them. Their primary responsibility to their subject is to seek and to state the truth as they see it. To this end professors devote their energies to developing and improving their scholarly competence. They accept the obligation to exercise critical self-discipline and judgment in using, extending, and transmitting knowledge. They practice intellectual honesty. Although professors may follow subsidiary interests, these interests must never seriously hamper or compromise their freedom of inquiry.

II. As teachers, professors encourage the free pursuit of learning in their students. They hold before them the best scholarly and ethical standards of their discipline. Professors demonstrate respect for students as individuals and adhere to their proper roles as intellectual guides and counselors. Professors make every reasonable effort to foster honest academic conduct and to ensure that their evaluations of students reflect each student's true merit. They respect the confidential nature of the relationship between professor and student. They avoid any exploitation, harassment, or discriminatory treatment of students. They acknowledge significant academic or scholarly assistance from them. They protect their academic freedom.

III. As colleagues, professors have obligations that derive from common membership in the community of scholars. Professors do not discriminate against or harass colleagues. They respect and defend the free inquiry of associates. In the exchange of criticism and ideas professors show due repect for the opinions of others. Professors acknowledge academic debt and strive to be objective in the professional judgment of colleagues. Professors accept their share of faculty responsibilities for the governance of their institution.

IV. As members of an academic institution, professors seek above all to be effective teachers and scholars. Although professors observe the stated regulations of the institution, provided the regulations do not contravene academic freedom, they maintain their right to criticize and seek revision. Professors give due regard to their paramount responsibilities within their institution in determining the amount and character of work done outside it. When considering the interruption or termination of their service, professors recognize the effect of their decision upon the program of the institution and give due notice of their intentions.

V. As members of their community, professors have the rights and obligations of other citizens. Professors measure the urgency of these obligations in the light of their responsibilities to their subject, to their students, to their profession, and to their institution. When they speak or act as private persons they avoid creating the impression of speaking or acting for their college or university. As citizens engaged in a profession that depends upon freedom for its health and integrity, professors have a particular obligation to promote conditions of free inquiry and to further public understanding of academic freedom.

Appendix 3

Statement of Professional Ethics of Professors of the Modern Language Association of America

Preamble

As the members of the MLA, we constitute a community of teachers and scholars joined together to serve the larger society by promoting the study and teaching of the modern languages and literatures. At the heart of this enterprise is freedom of inquiry, which we ask of the society we serve. This freedom carries with it the responsibilities of professional conduct. We intend this statement to embody reasonable norms for ethical conduct in teaching, research, and related public service activities in the modern languages and literatures. The statement's governing premises are as follows:

1. The responsibility for protecting free inquiry lies first with tenured faculty members, who may be called on to speak out against unethical behavior or to defend the academic freedom of colleagues at any rank.

2. Tenured and nontenured faculty members alike have ethical obligations to students, colleagues, staff members, their institutions, their local communities, the profession at large, and society. Therefore, in the continuing evaluation of faculty members by their colleagues, the way in which those obligations are fulfilled is an appropriate area for review.[1]

3. Our integrity as teachers and scholars implies a commitment to be responsible in using evidence and developing arguments and to be fair in hearing and reading the arguments of both colleagues and students.

From *Profession* 92. New York: Modern Language Association, 1992, 75–78. Reprinted by permission of the MLA.

4. Free inquiry respects the diversity of the modes and objects of investigation, whether they are traditional or innovative. We should defend scholarly practices against unfounded attacks from within or outside our community.

5. Our teaching and inquiry must respect simultaneously the diversity of our own culture and that of the cultures we study.

6. Judgments of whether a line of inquiry is ultimately useful to society, colleagues, or students should not be used to limit the freedom of the scholar pursuing it.

7. As a community valuing free inquiry, we must be able to rely on the integrity and the good judgment of our members. For this reason, we should not

- exploit or discriminate against others on any grounds, including race, ethnic origin, religious creed, age, gender, and sexual preference
- plagiarize the work of others[2]
- sexually harass students, colleagues, or staff members[3]
- misuse confidential information
- use language that is prejudicial or gratuitously derogatory
- make capricious or arbitrary decisions affecting working conditions, professional status, or academic freedom
- practice deceit or fraud on the academic community or the public

Ethical Conduct in Academic Relationships

A. Obligations to Students[4]

1. Faculty members should represent to their students the values of free inquiry.

2. At the outset of each course, faculty members should provide the students with a statement on approaches to the course materials, on the goals of the course, and on the standards by which the students will be evaluated.

3. Faculty members should offer constructive and timely evaluation of students' work and specify the times and places when they are available to consult with students.

4. Student-teacher collaboration entails the same obligation as other kinds of research: faculty members should acknowledge appropriately any intellectual indebtedness.

5. Faculty members whose research in any way includes students as subjects must make clear the obligations, rewards, and consequences of

participation. Such relationships also impose on researchers a special responsibility to guard the students involved from any form of abuse, such as betrayal of confidentiality, and to protect them from research-related harm or discomfort.

6. Inasmuch as the teaching of language, writing, and literature not only involves comprehension of the course material but may also draw, more directly than some other subjects do, on students' intellectual and emotional experiences, faculty members, in devising requirements for written work and oral discussion, have an ethical responsibility to respect both students' privacy and their emotional and intellectual dignity.

7. Faculty members should keep confidential what they know about students' academic standing, personal lives, and political or religious views and should not exploit such personal knowledge.

8. Faculty members should provide unbiased, professional evaluation of students seeking admission to graduate study or applying for financial support.

9. Faculty members should provide direction to graduate students, should respect their scholarly interests, and should not exploit them for personal or professional ends. Faculty members should not expect graduate students to perform unremunerated or uncredited teaching, research, or personal duties.

10. Faculty members working with teaching assistants have a special responsibility to provide them with adequate preparation, continuing guidance, and informed evaluation.

11. Faculty members must weigh the academic performance of each graduate student on its merits.

12. In overseeing and responding to the work of graduate students, whether they are in courses or at the thesis or dissertation stage, advisers should periodically inform them of their standing in the programs.

13. Before graduate students begin searching for jobs, faculty members should provide them with adequate and timely counseling and should be prepared to write honest and constructive letters of recommendation. Under certain circumstances, a faculty member who entertains basic doubts either about a student's competence or about his or her own ability to evaluate the student fairly may wish to decline the task of furnishing such a letter.

B. Obligations to Colleagues

1. Faculty members should evaluate candidates for appointment, reappointment, promotion, or tenure on professional grounds and in ap-

propriate forums.[5] Likewise, such candidates should submit accuraté credentials and represent themselves honestly.

2. Tenured faculty members should participate in the institutional processes by which tenure-track faculty members are evaluated and apprised of their standing. Similarly, the appropriate faculty members should periodically and fairly evaluate all other categories of nontenured faculty members.[6]

3. The appropriate faculty members should inform candidates for promotion or tenure of their rights, of the criteria germane to the evaluation, and of the methods by which the evaluation will be undertaken.

4. Faculty members on committees reviewing colleagues should keep confidential all information about persons under evaluation, not only in promotion and tenure reviews but also in reviews of chairs, searches for departmental administrators, and other such processes.

5. Faculty members in positions of leadership should assist their institutions in devising and implementing policies and procedures that promote a positive working environment. These policies and procedures should, for example, protect tenured and nontenured faculty members alike from any form of exploitation and provide all faculty members with a system for orderly and dignified retirement from full-time academic duties.

6. Faculty members should encourage the development of departmental and institutional policies that extend courtesies and specified privileges to independent scholars.

C. Obligations to Staff Members

1. Faculty members should value staff members as coworkers and, accordingly, should not require them to do inappropriate, unreasonable, unhealthy, or hazardous work.

2. Faculty members should recognize that the use of sexist or racist epithets or the repeated refusal to name a staff member according to his or her wishes constitutes a form of harassment.

3. Faculty members who supervise staff members should work to ensure that other faculty members and graduate students treat those staff members appropriately.

D. Obligations to the Institution and to the Local Community

1. Faculty members should support ethical behavior and protect academic freedom within their institutions.

2. Faculty members should be aware of how the policies, programs, and expansions of their institutions may affect local communities, par-

ticularly in matters in which modern language professionals may have a special competence, such as literacy.

3. Faculty members should ensure that their personal activities in politics and in their local communities remain distinct from any positions taken by their universities or colleges. They should avoid appearing to speak for their institutions when acting privately.

4. A faculty member planning to resign should give timely, written notice of this intention in accordance with university regulations. Until the existing appointment ends, he or she should not accept another appointment involving concurrent obligations without the permission of the appropriate administrator.

E. Obligations to the Profession at Large and to Society

1. In contributing to the profession at large, scholars should not accept assignments that they know they cannot carry out responsibly.

2. As referees for presses, journals, and promotion and tenure committees, scholars should judge the work of others fairly and in an informed way and should avoid any conflict of interest. A reader who is so out of sympathy with the author, topic, or critical stance of a work as to be unable to judge its merits without prejudice should decline to review it. Likewise, any referee with a personal relationship that prevents an unbiased evaluation should turn down the invitation to serve.

3. A scholar asked by an editor to evaluate a manuscript or book that the scholar has previously reviewed should inform the editor of the coincidence.

4. Referees should be fully informed of the evaluation procedures and should be allowed anonymity, unless there are legal requirements of disclosure.

5. The timetable for publication review should be made clear to both referees and authors. Referees should discharge their tasks in a timely manner; they should decline invitations whose deadlines they cannot meet. Editors should not use referees who habitually prolong the evaluation process. Any changes in a publication schedule should be conveyed promptly to the author involved. Undue delay in review or publication justifies the author to submit the manuscript to another outlet, provided the first editor is informed in writing.

6. A scholar who feels it necessary to submit work to more than one outlet simultaneously should so inform the editors receiving the submission.

7. A scholar who borrows from the works and ideas of others, including those of students, should acknowledge the debt, whether or not the sources are published. Unpublished scholarly material—which may

be encountered when it is read aloud, circulated in manuscript, or discussed—is especially vulnerable to unacknowledged appropriation, since the lack of a printed text makes originality hard to establish.

8. In communicating the principles and findings of their research to the public, scholars are obliged to be as accurate in their utterances as they are in addressing the academic community.

Conclusion

Our focus in this document is on the affirmative obligations of the modern language profession. Accountable as we are to the various groups and individuals listed here, we hold the view that a common understanding of our obligations to them will enable us both to exert appropriate restraints in exercising our responsibilities as scholars and teachers and to promote ethical behavior among our colleagues and among those who will follow us in the profession.

Notes

1. When a faculty member's fulfillment of ethical obligations is reviewed, care should be taken that it, like other subjects of evaluation, is not arbitrarily or capriciously judged. Any actions that may lead to the nonrenewal of an appointment, to the dismissal of a tenured faculty member, or to other such sanctions should be pursued in accordance with generally accepted procedural standards. See especially the "1940 Statement of Principles on Academic Freedom and Tenure" of the American Association of University Professors, endorsed by the MLA in 1962 and augmented with interpretive comments in 1970, and the related AAUP "Recommended Institutional Regulations on Academic Freedom and Tenure."

2. In this statement we adopt the definition of plagiarism given in *The MLA Style Manual:* "Plagiarism is the use of another person's ideas or expressions in your writing without acknowledging the source. . . . The most blatant form of plagiarism is reproducing someone else's sentences, more or less verbatim, and presenting them as your own. Other forms include repeating another's particularly apt phrase without appropriate acknowledgment, paraphrasing someone else's argument as your own, introducing another's line of thinking as your own development of an idea, and failing to cite the source for a borrowed thesis or approach" (Achtert and Gibaldi 1.4; cf. "What to Document," 5.1). It is important to note that this definition does not distinguish between published and unpublished sources, between ideas derived from colleagues and those offered by students, or between written and oral presentations.

3. In defining sexual harassment, we drew on statements such as the following: (1) "Sexual harassment is defined by law and includes any unwanted sexual

gesture, physical contact, or statement which is offensive, humiliating, or an interference with required tasks or career opportunities" ("Sexual Harassment"). (2) "Sexual harassment may be broadly defined as any unsolicited or objectionable emphasis on the sexuality or sexual identity of another person (whether student, colleague or employee) that might limit that individual's full participation in the academic community. This includes not only sexual advances, requests for sexual favors, or sexual assault, but also sexist remarks or jokes" (American Philological Association). (3) Conduct that is sexually harassing "interferes with an individual's work or academic performance [or] creates an intimidating, hostile or offensive working or academic environment" (Canadian Association 25-7).

4. For further development of some of the issues treated in this section, see the "Joint Statement on Rights and Freedoms of Students," prepared in 1967 by the AAUP and four other associations representing both students and student personnel administrators.

5. For more detailed recommendations on hiring, see Showalter.

6. We allude here both to part-time faculty members and to nontenure-track full-time faculty members. For further policy on the first group, see the guidelines set forth in the MLA's "Statement on the Use of Part-Time Faculty," adopted in 1982.

7. For a related statement on journal publications, see *Guidelines for Journal Editors and Contributors,* by the Conference of Editors of Learned Journals.

Works Cited

Achtert, Walter S., and Joseph Gibaldi. *The MLA Style Manual.* New York: MLA, 1985.

American Association of University Professors. *Policy Documents and Reports.* Washington: AAUP, 1990.

American Philological Association. "Statement on Professional Ethics." *Directory of Membership.* 8th ed. Atlanta: Scholars, 1991. N. pag.

Canadian Association of University Teachers. "Policy Statement on Professional Rights, Responsibilities and Relationships." *CAUT Information Service.* Ottawa: CAUT, n.d. 25-1–25-10.

Conference of Editors of Learned Journals. *Guidelines for Journal Editors and Contributors.* New York: MLA, 1984.

"Joint Statement on Rights and Freedoms of Students." American Association, *Policy Documents* 153–58.

Modern Language Association. "Statement on the Use of Part-Time Faculty." *ADE Bulletin* 74 (1983): 65. Rpt. annually in Oct. issues of *Job Information List,* English and foreign lang. eds., beginning 1982.

"1940 Statement of Principles on Academic Freedom and Tenure. With 1970 Interpretive Comments." American Association, *Policy Documents* 3–7.

"Recommended Institutional Regulations on Academic Freedom and Tenure." American Association, *Policy Documents* 21–30.

"Sexual Harassment." *The Faculty/Staff Handbook of the University of Illinois at Chicago, 1990–1992.* Chicago: U of Illinois, Chicago, n.d. 105.

Showalter, English. *A Career Guide for PhDs and PhD Candidates in English and Foreign Languages.* New York: MLA, 1985.

Appendix 4

Statement of Good Practices by Law Professors in the Discharge of Their Ethical and Professional Responsibilities

American law professors typically are members of two professions and thus should comply with the requirements and standards of each. Law professors who are lawyers are subject to the law of professional ethics in force in the relevant jurisdictions. Non-lawyers, in turn, should be guided by the norms associated with their disciplines. In addition, as members of the teaching profession, all law faculty members are subject to the regulations of the institutions at which they teach and to guidelines that are more generally applicable, such as the Statement on Professional Ethics of the American Association of University Professors.

This statement does not diminish the commands of other sources of ethical and professional conduct. Instead, it is intended to provide general guidance to law professors concerning ethical and professional standards both because of the intrinsic importance of those standards and because law professors serve as important role models for law students. In the words of the American Bar Association's Commission on Professionalism, since "the law school experience provides the student's first exposure to the profession and . . . professors inevitably serve as important role models for students, . . . the highest standards of ethics and professionalism should be adhered to within law schools."*

Law professors' responsibilities extend beyond the classroom to include out of class associations with students and other professional ac-

---

Washington, D.C.: Association of American Law Schools, 1996. Reprinted by permission of the AALS.

*". . . In the Spirit of Public Service:" A Blueprint for the Rekindling of Lawyer Professionalism 19 (1986).

tivities. Members of the law teaching profession should have a strong sense of the special obligations that attach to their calling. They should recognize their responsibility to serve others and not be limited to pursuit of self interest. This general aspiration cannot be achieved by edict, for moral integrity and dedication to the welfare of others cannot be legislated. Nevertheless, a public statement of good practices concerning ethical and professional responsibility can enlighten newcomers and remind experienced teachers about the basic ethical and professional tenets—the *ethos*—of their profession.

Although the norms of conduct set forth in this Statement may be relevant when questions concerning propriety of conduct arise in a particular institutional context, the statement is not promulgated as a disciplinary code. Rather, the primary purpose of the Statement—couched for the most part in general aspirational terms—is to provide guidance to law professors concerning their responsibilities (1) to students, (2) as scholars, (3) to colleagues, (4) to the law school and university at which they teach, and (5) to the bar and the general public.

I. Responsibilities to Students

As teachers, scholars, counselors, mentors, and friends, law professors can profoundly influence students' attitudes concerning professional competence and responsibility. Professors should assist students to recognize the responsibility of lawyers to advance individual and social justice.

Because of their inevitable function as role models, professors should be guided by the most sensitive ethical and professional standards.

Law professors should aspire to excellence in teaching and to mastery of the doctrines and theories of their subjects. They should prepare conscientiously for class and employ teaching methods appropriate for the subject matters and objectives of their courses. The objectives and requirements of their courses, including applicable attendance and grading rules, should be clearly stated. Classes should be met as scheduled or, when this is impracticable, classes should be rescheduled at a time reasonably convenient for students, or alternative means of instruction should be provided.

Law professors have an obligation to treat students with civility and respect and to foster a stimulating and productive learning environment in which the pros and cons of debatable issues are fairly acknowledged. Teachers should nurture and protect intellectual freedom for their students and colleagues. If a professor expresses views in class that were espoused in representing a client or in consulting, the professor should make appropriate disclosure.

Evaluation of student work is one of the fundamental obligations of law professors. Examinations and assignments should be conscientiously designed and all student work should be evaluated with impartiality. Grading should be done in a timely fashion and should be consistent with standards recognized as legitimate within the university and the profession. A student who so requests should be given an explanation of the grade assigned.

Law professors should be reasonably available to counsel students about academic matters, career choices, and professional interests. In performing this function, professors should make every reasonable effort to ensure that the information they transmit is timely and accurate. When in the course of counseling a law professor receives information that the student may reasonably expect to be confidential, the professor should not disclose that information unless required to do so by university rule or applicable law. Professors should inform students concerning the possibility of such disclosure.

Professors should be as fair and complete as possible when communicating evaluative recommendations for students and should not permit invidious or irrelevant considerations to infect these recommendations. If information disclosed in confidence by the student to the professor makes it impossible for the professor to write a fair and complete recommendation without revealing the information, the professor should so inform the student and refuse to provide the recommendation unless the student consents to full disclosure.

Discriminatory conduct based on such factors as race, color, religion, national origin, sex, sexual orientation, disability or handicap, age, or political beliefs is unacceptable in the law school community. Law professors should seek to make the law school a hospitable community for all students and should be sensitive to the harmful consequences of professorial or student conduct or comments in classroom discussions or elsewhere that perpetuate stereotypes or prejudices involving such factors. Law professors should not sexually harass students and should not use their role or position to induce a student to enter into a sexual relationship, or to subject a student to a hostile academic environment based on any form of sexual harassment.

Sexual relationships between a professor and a student who are not married to each other or who do not have a preexisting analogous relationship are inappropriate whenever the professor has a professional responsibility for the student in such matters as teaching a course or in otherwise evaluating, supervising, or advising a student as part of a school program. Even when a professor has no professional responsibility for a student, the professor should be sensitive to the perceptions of other students that a student who has a sexual relationship with a professor may receive preferential treatment from the professor or the professor's colleagues. A professor who is closely related to a student by blood or marriage, or who has a preexisting analogous relationship with a student, normally should eschew roles involving a professional responsibility for the student.

II. Responsibilities as Scholars

A basic responsibility of the community of higher education in the United States is to refine, extend, and transmit knowledge. As members of that community, law professors share with their colleagues in the other disciplines the obligation to discharge that responsibility. Law schools are required by accreditation standards to limit the burden of teaching so that professors will have the time to do research and to share its results with others. Law schools also have a responsibility to maintain an atmosphere of freedom and tolerance in which knowledge can be sought and shared without hindrance. Law professors are obligated, in turn, to make the best and fullest use of that freedom to fulfill their scholarly responsibilities.

In teaching, as well as in research, writing, and publication, the scholarship of others is indispensable to one's own. A law professor thus has a responsibility to be informed concerning the relevant scholarship of others in the fields in which the professor writes and teaches. To keep current in any field of law requires continuing study. To this extent the professor, as a scholar, must remain a student. As a corollary, law professors have a responsibility to engage in their own research and publish their conclusions. In this way, law professors participate in an intellectual exchange that tests and improves their knowledge of the field, to the ultimate benefit of their students, the profession, and society.

The scholar's commitment to truth requires intellectual honesty and open-mindedness. Although a law professor should feel free to criticize another's work, distortion or misrepresentation is always unacceptable. Relevant evidence and arguments should be addressed. Conclusions should be frankly stated, even if unpopular.

When another's scholarship is used—whether that of another professor or that of a student—it should be fairly summarized and candidly acknowledged. Significant contributions require acknowledgment in every context in which ideas are exchanged. Publication permits at least three ways of doing this: shared authorship, attribution by footnote or endnote, and discussion of another's contribution within the main text.

Which of these will suffice to acknowledge scholarly contributions by others will, of course, depend on the extent of the contribution.

A law professor has a responsibility to preserve the integrity and independence of legal scholarship. Sponsored or remunerated research should always be acknowledged with full disclosure of the interests of the parties. If views expressed in an article were also espoused in the course of representation of a client or in consulting, this should be acknowledged.

III. Responsibilities to Colleagues

Law professors should treat colleagues and staff members with civility and respect. Senior law professors should be particularly sensitive to the terms of any debate involving their junior colleagues and should so conduct themselves that junior colleagues will understand that no adverse professional consequences would follow from expression of, or action based upon, beliefs or opinions contrary to those held by the senior professor.

Matters of law school governance deserve the exercise of independent judgment by each voting member of the faculty. It is therefore inappropriate for a law professor to apply any sort of pressure other than persuasion on the merits in an effort to influence the vote of another member of the faculty.

Law professors should comply with institutional rules or policies requiring confidentiality concerning oral or written communications. Such rules or policies frequently will exist with respect to personnel matters and evaluations of student performance. If there is doubt whether such a rule or policy is in effect, a law professor should seek clarification.

An evaluation made of any colleague for purposes of promotion or tenure should be based exclusively upon appropriate academic and service criteria fairly weighted in accordance with standards understood by the faculty and communicated to the subject of the evaluation.

Law professors should make themselves reasonably available to colleagues for purposes of discussing teaching methods, content of courses, possible topics of scholarship, scholarly work in progress, and related matters. Except in rare cases and for compelling reasons, professors should always honor requests from their own law schools for evaluation of scholarship in connection with promotion or tenure decisions. Law professors should also give sympathetic consideration to similar requests from other law schools.

As is the case with respect to students (Part I), sexual harassment, or discriminatory conduct involving colleagues or staff members on the basis of race, color, religion, national origin, sex, sexual orientation, disability or handicap, age, or political beliefs is unacceptable.

IV. Responsibilities to the Law School and University

Law professors have a responsibility to participate in the governance of their university and particularly the law school itself. Although many duties within modern universities are assumed by professional administrators, the faculty retains substantial collective responsibility to provide institutional leadership. Individual professors have a responsibility to assume a fair share of that leadership, including the duty to serve on faculty committees and to participate in faculty deliberations.

Law professors are frequently in demand to participate in activities outside the law school. Such involvement may help bring fresh insights to the professor's classes and writing. Excessive involvement in outside activities, however, tends to reduce the time that the professor has to meet obligations to students, colleagues, and the law school. A professor thus has a responsibility both to adhere to a university's specific limitations on outside activity and to assure that outside activities do not significantly diminish the professor's availability to meet institutional obligations. Professors should comply with applicable laws and university regulations and policies concerning the use of university funds, personnel, and property in connection with such activities.

When a law professor resigns from the university to assume another position, or seeks a leave of absence to teach at another institution, or assumes a temporary position in practice or government, the professor should provide reasonable advance notice. Absent unusual circumstances, a professor should adhere to the dates established in the Statement of Good Practices for the Recruitment of and Resignation by Full-Time Faculty Members of the Association of American Law Schools.

Although all law professors have the right as citizens to take positions on public questions, each professor has a duty not to imply that he or she speaks on behalf of the law school or university. Thus, a professor should take steps to assure that any designation of the professor's institution in connection with the professor's name is for identification only.

V. Responsibilities to the Bar and General Public

A law professor occupies a unique role as a bridge between the bar and students preparing to become members of the bar. It is important that professors accept the responsibilities of professional status. At a minimum, a law professor should adhere to the Code or Rules of Professional Conduct of the state bars to which the law professor may belong. A law professor may responsibly test the limits of professional rules in an effort to determine their constitutionality or proper application. Other conduct warranting discipline as a lawyer should be a matter of serious concern to the professor's law school and university.

One of the traditional obligations of members of the bar is to engage in uncompensated public service or pro bono legal activities. As role models for students and as members of the legal profession, law professors share this responsibility. This responsibility can be met in a variety of ways, including direct client contact through legal aid or public defender offices (whether or not through the law school), participating in the legal work of public interest organizations, lecturing in continuing legal education programs, educating public school pupils or other groups concerning the legal system, advising local, state, and national government officials on legal issues, engaging in legislative drafting, or other law reform activities.

The fact that a law professor's income does not depend on serving the interests of private clients permits a law professor to take positions on issues as to which practicing lawyers may be more inhibited. With that freedom from economic pressure goes an enhanced obligation to pursue individual and social justice.

Adopted by the Executive Committee
November 17, 1989

Appendix 5

On Teaching

(A) *The Teaching Portfolio: A Checklist of Items That Might Be Included*

Faculty members should recognize which of the items which might be included in a teaching dossier would most effectively give a favorable impression of teaching competence and which might better be used for self-evaluation and improvement. The dossier should be compiled to make the best possible case for teaching effectiveness.

The Products of Good Teaching

1. Students' scores on teacher-made or standardized tests, possibly before and after a course has been taken as evidence of learning.
2. Student laboratory workbooks and other kinds of workbooks or logs.
3. Student essays, creative work, and project or field-work reports.
4. Publications by students on course-related work.
5. A record of students who select and succeed in advanced courses of study in the field.
6. A record of students who elect another course with the same professor.
7. Evidence of effective supervision of Honors, Master's or Ph.D. theses.

From B. M. Shore et al. *The Teaching Dossier: A Guide to Its Preparation and Use.* Revised edition. Montreal: Canadian Association of University Teachers, 1986. Reprinted in Russell Edgerton, Patricia Hutchings, and Kathleen Quinlan. *The Teaching Portfolio: Capturing the Scholarship in Teaching.* Washington, D.C.: American Association for Higher Education, 1991, 8. Reprinted by permission of the Canadian Association of University Teachers.

8. Setting up or running a successful internship program.

9. Documentary evidence of the effect of courses on student career choice.

10. Documentary evidence of help given by the professor to students in securing employment.

11. Evidence of help given to colleagues on teaching improvement.

Material from Oneself

Descriptive material on current and recent teaching responsibilities and practices.

12. List of course titles and numbers, unit values or credits, enrollments with brief elaboration.

13. List of course materials prepared for students.

14. Information on professor's availability to students.

15. Report on identification of student difficulties and encouragement of student participation in courses or programs.

16. Description of how films, computers or other nonprint materials were used in teaching.

17. Steps taken to emphasize the interrelatedness and relevance of different kinds of learning.

Description of steps taken to evaluate and improve one's teaching.

18. Maintaining a record of the changes resulting from self-evaluation.

19. Reading journals on improving teaching and attempting to implement acquired ideas.

20. Reviewing new teaching materials for possible application.

21. Exchanging course materials with a colleague from another institution.

22. Conducting research on one's own teaching or course.

23. Becoming involved in an association or society concerned with the improvement of teaching and learning.

24. Attempting instructional innovations and evaluating their effectiveness.

25. Using general support services such as the Education Resources Information Centre (ERIC) in improving one's teaching.

26. Participating in seminars, workshops and professional meetings intended to improve teaching.

27. Participating in course or curriculum development.
28. Pursuing a line of research that contributes directly to teaching.
29. Preparing a textbook or other instructional materials.
30. Editing or contributing to a professional journal on teaching one's subject.

Information from Others

Students:

31. Student course and teaching evaluation data which suggest improvements or produce an overall rating of effectiveness or satisfaction.
32. Written comments from a student committee to evaluate courses and provide feedback.
33. Unstructured (and possibly unsolicited) written evaluations by students, including written comments on exams and letters received after a course has been completed.
34. Documented reports of satisfaction with out-of-class contacts.
35. Interview data collected from students after completion of a course.
36. Honors received from students, such as being elected "teacher of the year."

Colleagues:

37. Statements from colleagues who have observed teaching either as members of a teaching team or as independent observers of a particular course, or who teach other sections of the same course.
38. Written comments from those who teach courses for which a particular course is a prerequisite.
39. Evaluation of contributions to course development and improvement.
40. Statements from colleagues from other institutions on such matters as how well students have been prepared for graduate studies.
41. Honors or recognition such as a distinguished teacher award or election to a committee on teaching.
42. Requests for advice or acknowledgement of advice received by a committee on teaching or similar body.

Other sources:

43. Statements about teaching achievements from administrators at one's own institution or from other institutions.

44. Alumni ratings or other graduate feedback.
45. Comments from parents of students.
46. Reports from employers of students (e.g., in a work-study or "cooperative" program).
47. Invitations to teach for outside agencies.
48. Invitations to contribute to the teaching literature.
49. Other kinds of invitations based on one's reputation as a teacher (for example, a media interview on a successful teaching innovation).

Appendix 5

On Teaching

(B) Teaching Circles

Even on campuses where good teaching is a top priority, faculty I talk with report an experience that Lee Shulman calls "pedagogical solitude"—a state of affairs in which that aspect of faculty work that would *seem* to be the most social, the most public, turns out in fact to be the most unrelievedly private. Maybe there's occasional, desultory chat about teaching in the elevator or faculty dining room, but when it comes to planned, purposeful conversation—occasions *set aside* for good talk about good teaching (and meaningful student learning)—the situation is pretty bleak. In such circumstances, teaching circles are a wonderful way to get the conversation started.

• • •

Fostering Collective Responsibility for Student Learning: Teaching Seminars in the University of North Carolina at Charlotte Mathematics Department

by Charles Burnap and Miriam Leiva, Faculty Members, Department of Mathematics, University of North Carolina at Charlotte

Last year, in order to begin a departmental conversation about teaching and learning, we held teaching seminars approximately once a month. The seminars were open to all mathematics faculty members— approximately forty to forty-five people—and attendance ranged be-

From Pat Hutchings. *Making Teaching Community Property: A Menu for Peer Collaboration and Peer Review.* Washington, D.C.: American Association for Higher Education, 1996, 7, 10–12. Reprinted by permission of Charles Burnap and Miriam Leiva and the AAHE.

tween ten and twenty people, depending on the topic and time of year. A core population of eight to ten individuals attended every (or almost every) seminar. As always, refreshments, including pizza, were served to encourage participation.

Most of our teaching seminars began with a series of questions designed to stimulate discussion on a particular teaching-related topic, which was announced in advance. However, it's important to say that once the seminar was under way, the discussion was shaped by participants' interests, and we didn't feel constrained to deal with each question on our list. As much as possible, the two of us tried to act as facilitators and not as directors.

After each seminar, we distributed discussion summaries to all mathematics faculty members (not just those who attended the seminar).

Seminar I: a focus on the department's goals for student learning

For our first seminar, we decided to focus on common goals in the teaching of mathematics—a prerequisite to eventual discussions about what constitutes good teaching practice. The first step, that is, was trying to determine what we, as a department, are trying to accomplish. We began the dialogue by asking the following questions:

1) In what ways do you teach students how mathematicians work?
2) Teaching students to reason is a goal in mathematics instruction. What are the other goals in teaching mathematics?
3) How important is it to make connections between your courses and other courses in mathematics? In other disciplines?
4) How important is it to discuss how and why a given area of mathematics was developed?
5) How important is self-discovery for students?
6) What are your concerns about teaching?

Naturally, we weren't able to address all these questions, but we did manage to generate a preliminary list of departmental goals for students' learning. We wish to help students to:

- Reason mathematically.
- Develop logical thought and critical thinking.
- Become mathematics problem solvers.
- Understand whether the results obtained are reasonable.
- Make bridges to abstractions.
- Recognize key mathematical concepts and skills.
- Distinguish between routine problems and those requiring creativity.

- Know and use mathematical language and procedures.
- Be able to communicate mathematically.
- Apply mathematical skills and knowledge in other subject areas, especially within the student's own discipline.

Seminars II and III: a focus on achieving our goals for student learning

For the next teaching seminar, we decided to focus on strategies that would help us implement the goals determined during the previous seminar. We began the discussion with two broad questions:

1) What are your concerns about teaching?
2) What specific suggestions/ideas/strategies do you have that may help us with our teaching?

The ensuing discussion was highly productive—if not always clearly focused on the goals. In the second seminar, the group talked about ways of encouraging student involvement, the formation of student study groups, and strategies for dealing with discipline problems such as students' talking during class, arriving late, and/or leaving early.

The third seminar also centered on achieving our goals, and we used the same two prompt questions. By this time, topics for discussion seemed to arise naturally. We even got into issues related to assessment, which many faculty identified as "a concern." We decided, then, to take assessment as the core topic for our fourth seminar.

Seminar IV: a focus on assessing student learning

Once again we posed a series of questions to guide the seminar discussion:

1) What we assess and how we assess it communicates what we value. A good assessment instrument should emphasize the mathematics that is most important for students to learn. What points should be emphasized?
2) Mathematics instruction and assessment should be linked so that each one reinforces the other. How can we use assessment to enhance our instruction?
3) Assessment should provide an opportunity for students to evaluate and improve their work. Does our assessment process actually result in improved performance?
4) Assessment should allow students to further their learning. Is it important to include nonroutine/open-ended problems on tests?

5) The validity of assessment is a characteristic not of the instrument itself but rather of the inferences made on the basis of the assessment. What can we learn from tests, quizzes, and homework problems?

6) Valid inferences are based on multiple sources of evidence. What methods can we use to evaluate student work?

Outcomes and benefits of our teaching seminars

Comments from participants indicate that the teaching seminars were helpful to many individuals in the department, especially those who attended regularly. In general, there was a sense that the seminars fostered more conversation about teaching. One person noted, "It was useful to exchange ideas on teaching philosophy and practices. While we might not all agree on every detail, it is important to have this type of discussion." Another said, "This was a real eye-opener. I realized we were a *group* of mathematicians, but that we don't usually cooperate on our teaching efforts."

The impact of the seminars on departmental culture is harder to know, but one outcome is that there is now a core of a dozen or so individuals (out of a department of forty to forty-five) who want to continue the discussion about learning goals and teaching practices. Additionally, at the request of several graduate students, we have now begun a series of teaching seminars designed to help our teaching assistants.

Plans for a next stage of work

We will continue to promote a dialogue about teaching within our department, but many participants in the seminars feel that it is now time to channel our efforts into discussions directed toward specific courses or groups of courses. As a starting point for these discussions, we could use the course files that we have established. We could also try to take advantage of some existing administrative structures: The department has recently established a Calculus Sequence Committee (charged with overseeing our implementation of reformed calculus material) and a Differential Equations Committee (charged with overseeing an introductory differential equations course).

Looking back, we are pleased with the seminars strategy. We considered other options for departmental action but felt that we could best build faculty involvement by taking advantage of the extensive discussion of teaching goals and practices within the mathematics education literature. By drawing on this material we provided a framework that was also an icebreaker.

Appendix 5

On Teaching

(C) Considering Teaching in the Appointment of Faculty Members

The Pedagogical Colloquium: Focusing on Teaching in the Hiring Process in the Stanford University History Department

by Richard Roberts, Faculty Member, Department of History, Stanford University

One of the results of participation in AAHE's peer review of teaching project was that I put forward to the history department a set of suggestions for raising the level of attention to teaching. One suggestion focused on the fact that the department was about to embark on three or four searches, and we saw an opportunity to get our candidates to talk about teaching in a way that hadn't been possible in our previous context of the "job talk" as a formal lecture on the candidate's research interest. The research presentation had served us well in giving a sense of the candidate's intellectual reach, but it was not at all clear that it was a sufficient test of the capacity to teach in a variety of settings.

Our purpose

What we did, then, was to propose that all our candidates engage not only in the traditional job talk but in an "informal discussion about teaching and curriculum"—a phrase we chose because the more formal "pedagogical colloquium" label raised concerns among my colleagues that they themselves did not have a clearly defined theory of teaching or

From Pat Hutchings. *Making Teaching Community Property: A Menu for Peer Collaboration and Peer Review.* Washington, D.C.: American Association for Higher Education, 1996, 83–85. Reprinted by permission of Richard Roberts and the AAHE.

pedagogy, and that there was no way we could ask freshly minted PhDs to lay out their philosophy of teaching in formal, theoretical terms.

Our aim was to assess in our "informal discussion" the degree to which candidates were actively engaged with teaching and how they thought about making available to students the kinds of intellectual interests in the field that they themselves were pursuing as scholars.

How we ran our "informal discussion about teaching and curriculum"

Candidates were told in advance that this new pedagogical discussion would take place; they were encouraged to prepare for it by putting together syllabi for courses they might teach and to take a look at the curriculum we offer. What we wanted to do was to see how candidates would fit into the teaching enterprise that we already have, and how they would build on and contribute to it.

The discussion lasted an hour and a half. We began by asking about courses the candidate would want to teach, and ranged, from there, to questions about teaching graduates and undergraduates, and about how the courses he or she might propose would fit into the Stanford curriculum.

We were especially interested in the candidate's comments on how he or she would teach a particular book—or sequence of books, or methodological debate—which was *very* revealing.

Impact on the hiring process

First, let me say that the candidates themselves—even one who had very little teaching experience—thought the pedagogical discussion was a terrific idea.

My colleagues, too, were largely persuaded. While at the outset they rather grudgingly accepted this addition to the usual job talk, it was clear that the new occasion provided important information that the department considered in making appointments. For instance, there was one candidate who gave a good—a very good—job talk; the research was really very well honed. But when it came to talking about teaching, it became clear that this candidate had put very little time into thinking about teaching. The search committee took this information into consideration when advancing a finalist to the department.

In another case, the teaching discussion kept a candidate in the running when the job talk was less than stupendous.

Impact on the culture of the department

First, the new discussion of teaching and curriculum was an occasion for important conversation among department members—especially as we evaluated candidates—that had not regularly occurred in the past. One of the most important aspects of the experience was the excitement on the part of faculty attending the discussion.

Second, the experience was good for our graduate students, who were encouraged to attend. They saw our candidates as potential teachers whose abilities they could evaluate, and, perhaps more important, they saw that talking about teaching and being thoughtful about it was one of the kinds of things that is likely to be expected of *them* when they go on the job market.

With this in mind, I'm introducing a series of workshops for graduate students to help them prepare for the job market—helping them put together materials about their teaching that will be useful in searches.

Issues to consider

One issue we were very concerned about was that our "informal discussion" not discriminate against candidates who had—through no fault of their own—little teaching experience. We didn't want to favor only those who had several years of teaching experience and could talk more eloquently about it. This turned out not to be a problem in the case of one candidate who had done almost no teaching but who had prepared wonderfully for the discussion and did a superb job of talking about the kinds of teaching that she would like to do. Nevertheless, this is probably an issue to keep in mind in the future, and to stay vigilant about.

Next steps

We have another series of searches coming up, and my expectation is that we will continue to employ the "informal discussion about teaching and curriculum" as part of the search process. It was instituted as a departmental experiment, so we'll revisit the topic, but my sense is that we'll stay with it.

The real question for the future, though, is how sustained the change will be—what linkages the search process will have with the culture of the department. Frankly, I'm doubtful that it will have any sustained impact without systematic follow-through, which means attention to teaching not just at the moment of hire but beyond that, through the ways it is evaluated for instance . . . and that will require stronger signals from upper-level administration. Without such signals, teaching will continue to be seen by many faculty in the department as a private, individual activity, not as a central aspect of the wider university culture.

Appendix 6

Scholars Fear "Star" System May Undercut Their Mission

Janny Scott

Collectors bid on Picassos, baseball teams bid on batters, television networks bid on prime-time shows. Now, in the era of academic free agency, a few dozen top universities vie with increasing intensity for much admired, much resented "academostars."

Bidding wars break out regularly over molecular biologists, African-American historians, mathematicians, whoever university administrators believe possess the reputation and scholarly heft to lift a department or a school up a rung in the national rankings.

They cast their bids in the arcane currency of academic compensation: not just salary, but also course load, research assistance, laboratory space, semesters off, housing subsidies, travel budgets, jobs for spouses (and even, in one case, a job for a former spouse in a joint-custody divorce).

"It's very much a part of the late 20th century, this celebrity-itis," said Joyce Appleby, a professor of history at the University of California at Los Angeles. "It is the academic aspect of the fascination with instant gratification, competition and races for prestige and celebrity status."

Consider the middle-aged associate professor at a reputable state university, earning a perfectly respectable $43,000 a year. When his book became a finalist for two of the top prizes in his field, he was catapulted into the giddy world of academic stardom.

First, even before the book was out, his university promoted him and

---

The New York Times, December 20, 1997, A1, A18. Copyright © 1997 by the New York Times Co. Reprinted by permission.

gave him a $10,000 raise. Then a top private university offered him an additional $25,000, a reduced teaching load, tuition for his children and guaranteed paid leave if he would defect.

His university countered, more or less matching the offer. So the professor decided not to leave. The next year, two Ivy League schools approached him, promising $15,000 more. Again, his university matched the offers. After some soul-searching, he stayed, feeling exhilarated but guilty.

"I'm simultaneously proud and embarrassed," said the professor, who spoke on condition that he not be identified. "You can't double your salary in two or three years and not think, 'Am I that much smarter than I was two or three years ago?' "

There is nothing new, of course, about academics with national reputations. What has changed is the competition for their services. Top universities have stepped up their longtime efforts to lure good people from lesser schools, while upwardly mobile, lesser schools have joined the fray.

What they are hunting for are scholars with big names in their field, people who win fellowships, publish prize-winning books, redefine their subjects, professors like Edward Said at Columbia, Henry Louis Gates Jr. and Cornel West at Harvard, or Judith Butler at the University of California at Berkeley.

Now Ms. Appleby is one of a number of scholars who have begun making the case in recent months that the star system is poisoning academic life, widening the gulf between the haves and have-nots and undermining the ideal of parity they say is basic to building community and morale.

The system rewards trendiness over less flashy virtues, critics say; it devalues the more ordinary hard work of academic life; it adds pressure on universities to do even more fund-raising, subtly eroding their independence, and it diverts attention from scholarship to the prestige attached to it.

Now that outside offers have become the route to a pay raise at home, some professors seem to flirt perpetually with suitors. That practice, critics say, breeds disloyalty, alienation and an insidious form of keeping up with the Joneses.

"There is a lot of low-level complaining and bitterness on many campuses about stars," said Cary Nelson, a professor of liberal arts and sciences at the University of Illinois at Urbana-Champaign, who published an article about academic superstars in the magazine Academe earlier this year. "But academia has not found a good way to discuss them openly. There's a tremendous amount of ill will but not a lot of open confrontation."

At the same time, many scholars concede that the star system can work. They say most stars are brilliant and highly productive; they have the power to attract gifted graduate students, reinvigorate departments, improve rankings, make alumni proud and make it easier to raise money.

• • •

"The sheer number of academic stars is the principal determinant of the public's assessment of the quality of a department," said Jonathan Cole, the Columbia University provost. "In academic life, you're known for your best, not for your average."

The star system can be traced, in part, to economic pressures squeezing universities and the pervasiveness of marketing in American life. Some specifically blame the preoccupation of administrators with rankings done by academic groups and publications like *U.S. News & World Report.*

But something else has changed, too. David R. Shumway, an associate professor in the English department at Carnegie Mellon University, says that the rise of the conference and lecture circuits has helped create a new form of academic celebrity akin to movie and rock stardom.

In a paper published in January in the journal Publications of the Modern Language Association, Mr. Shumway described Jacques Derrida, the father of deconstruction, as "*the* jet-set academic, a professor who seems to spend more time in the air between gigs than on the ground at any particular job."

Long magazine profiles illustrated with photographs of tousled scholars in black turtlenecks have helped personalize their images, Mr. Shumway suggested. And recent trends in scholarship have placed issues like gender and sexuality at the center of certain fields.

"One might hazard a guess that the public visibility of the stars in some ways came about because it was the way the press preferred to deal with them," Mr. Shumway said, "rather than to engage the difficult and arcane matters that they actually write about."

Who becomes a "poster professor," as the new breed has been called by Jeffrey Williams, a professor of English at East Carolina University who also coined the term academostar? Most tend to be in their 40's and 50's and in mid-career; their research is cutting-edge; many are in trendy fields like environmental history or ethnic studies with a lot of student interest and not enough teachers.

Visibility helps. Stars write articles that regularly make a splash. They appear at conferences, where they are often used to draw a crowd. Some write for mainstream publications like *The New Yorker, The New Republic* and *The New York Review of Books.* Their books win important prizes.

• • •

Questioning A Market Model

More than any other reaction, the star system engenders mixed emotions. More power to anyone in a captive labor market who ends up well paid, some professors say; if stars bring a university fame, energy, better graduate students and good faculty, everyone benefits.

At the same time, many wonder whether the market is the wrong model for faculty recruiting. As Ms. Appleby put it, the market ignores qualities that universities value, like the nurturing of talents over a lifetime and the development of certain intellectual values.

"By adopting the market as a model, universities have turned recruitment into a national competition, much like college sports," she wrote in a recent column in a newsletter published by the American Historical Association, the historians' organization of which she is president.

"Where once universities relied upon their location, reputation, facilities and student body to attract new faculty members," she continued, "today they are spending university money on 'off-scale' salaries, negotiated promotions and reduced teaching loads that will drain budgets for years to come."

Appendix 7

The Theory of the Profession
and Its Predicament

Sanford H. Kadish

The AAUP over the years has relied upon a variety of means to bring its
influence to bear on higher education in the United States. It has prepared and disseminated an elegant body of position papers on central issues, it has sometimes had recourse to law suits, it has used the tech-
nique of publicity through publication of its *ad hoc* committee reports
and its censure lists. But underlying all of these modes of influence has
been an appeal to the entitlements of the professor. By this I mean an
assertion of claims justified in terms of their consistency with some
shared values transcending the personal interests of any single group.
Of course, most groups in society have recourse to claimed entitlements
as part of their assortment of means of influencing others. Need I mention Secretary Wilson's famous observation, "What is good for General
Motors is good for the country." But with the AAUP in its actions on
behalf of the profession, the appeal to entitlements has been central. Indeed, the Association probably owes its being to its founders' recognition of the need for an organization to articulate them.

This special mode of influence has entailed the development of a theory of the profession. I mean by this an integrated set of propositions
with respect to the nature of higher education, with respect to certain
shared values, and with respect to certain understandings of the roles of
the professor in the university and of the university in the larger community, all of which serve to support and justify a variety of profes-

AAUP Bulletin 58 (June 1972), 120–125. Reprinted by permission of the
American Association of University Professors.

sional claims, as well as correlative duties which the theory allows to be made against the professor.

The basic theme of my remarks today is that we are facing a predicament with respect to the theory; that its consistency and vitality are being subjected to substantial strains by the course of events in recent years, events inside and outside the Association; and that the predicament extends not just to the continued viability of the theory, but also to the very commitment of resting on a theory of the profession as a basis for advancing professional claims. I will try to develop that theme by 1) sketching the main tenets of that theory; 2) identifying the developments which threaten it; and 3) suggesting the terms in which resolutions should be sought.

The Association's Theory of the Profession

The Association's theory of the profession may be found in and between the lines of its papers and reports from 1915 to the present. That theory makes exceedingly bold claims.[1] Although relying for financial support on private benefactors or the public and justifying our existence in terms of the public good, we make the extraordinary claim that we should be left alone. Like the underlying point of a rambling letter one of us might receive from his or her youngster away from home, the theory says essentially: "Understand us, love us, send us money, and leave us to do our thing." And all this it asks for the public good and not that of the professor. When asked to explain why private benefactors, governmental agencies, and the public generally should establish for the professor this *imperium in imperio,* free of the controls imposed on other segments of democratic society—business, professional, industrial—our reply and our justification is our special theory of the profession.

The university, we say, is conducted for the common good and not to further the interest of either the individual teacher or the institution as a whole. That common good depends on the free search for truth and its expression[2] by trained specialists in investigation and reflection whose peculiar and necessary service requires that their views and conclusions be their own unquestioned products as people "trained for and dedicated to the quest for truth."[3] It follows therefore that professors must be allowed an academic freedom in their research and teaching in order to be free of restraints from inexpert or not wholly disinterested persons outside their ranks,[4] whether they be governors or legislators, regents or administrators. It follows also that the professor must be provided with security of tenure after a probationary period, in order further to protect this freedom of research and teaching and to assure a degree of economic security, both of which are indispensable to the success of an institution in fulfilling its obligations to its students and to society.[5] And it further follows that the university and the faculty as a collectivity are debarred from identifying with particular causes or particular views of what is true or of what is right—beyond the procedural commitment to freedom—lest an orthodoxy be imposed of greater or lesser extent which subverts the special university role. As Walter Metzger summarized the sense of the framers of the 1915 Declaration of Principles in this respect: "Intellectual inquiry, they insisted, had to be ongoing and individual; organizational fiats defeat it because organizations are weightier than individuals and fiats are inevitably premature. In support of their brief for neutrality they likened the true university to an 'intellectual experiment station' where new ideas might safely germinate, to an 'inviolable refuge' where men of ideas might safely congregate, and—most simply—to a 'home for research.' "[6]

And all of these claims we make "not as a special right, but as a means whereby we may make our appointed contribution to the life of the commonwealth,"[7] for we are members of a profession who are "dedicated above all else to the advancement of higher education and to the ideals of individual and corporate action which will best serve this advancement, and who conceive that their personal interests as members of the profession are to be defended and furthered only as subservient to this larger aim."[8]

This autonomy of the professor over his own research and teaching must for similar reasons be accompanied by a like autonomy of the faculty collectively with respect to the central educational decisions within the university—particularly curriculum and personnel decisions. Effectiveness in rendering the special services of the university in acquiring and transmitting knowledge requires that those decisions be made by the professors themselves, and this is true because it is they who possess the special training, competence, experience, special understanding, and professional commitment necessary for sound and reliable decisions.[9]

The bases of these claimed entitlements to freedom and autonomy also produce correlative obligations on the professor:[10] for example, that he carry on his work in the temper of scientific inquiry; that his conclusions be gained by a "scholar's method and held in a scholar's spirit";[11] that he encourage the free pursuit of learning in his students;[12] that in exercising his right over academic governance of his institutions he exercise objective professional judgment, defend free inquiry, and recognize his "direct professional obligations to . . . students, . . . colleagues, . . . discipline."[13]

But it is "inadmissible that the power of determining when departures from the requirements of the scientific spirit and method have occurred should be vested in bodies not composed of members of the academic profession. Such bodies necessarily lack full competence to judge of those requirements: their intervention can never be exempt from the suspicion that it is dictated by other motives than zeal for the integrity of science, ... It follows that university teachers must be prepared to assume this responsibility for themselves."[14]

All of this, of course, is familiar doctrine indeed. Let me in summary reemphasize three aspects of it. First, taken in the large its network of principles and assertions functions as a theory of the profession in terms of which we stake our claim of entitlement to academic freedom and tenure and to educational autonomy within the university. Second, the claims it makes for immunity from public control, in the face of its claims as well for public support and its justification of serving a public mission, are truly extraordinary. What other social institution, after all, presumes to make those claims? Commerce and industry once did, but today laissez-faire is a relic of the past. The judiciary still does, but subordinately to the power of political forces to amend the law or the Constitution. Churches have managed to stake out a comparable claim, but historically only at the cost of government support. Third, so far are those critics misguided who see only the hole of the doughnut in the substantial gaps between the assertion of this doctrine and its realization, that the extent to which this set of justifications for such audacious claims has come to be part of the prevailing ethos of higher education is truly remarkable. In fact, the theory has served us surprisingly well in advancing our freedom and our autonomy and we should lose a great deal if we allowed its authority to dissipate.

Cracks in the Theory

I turn now to some trends and movements in higher education today which collide with the premises underlying that theory and make it increasingly less coherent and persuasive as a basis for asserting our claims. This is the predicament of which I spoke earlier.

I see these trends and movements falling into three categories: the first has to do with claims of the professor as employee; the second, with claims in behalf of direct social involvement by the university and its faculty; the third, with the claims for the application of democratic political precepts in decision-making within the university. To capsulate: A. The Professor as Employee; B. The Professor and his University as Super-Citizen;[15] and C. The University as a Body Politic.

The Professor as Employee

It has been true for a long time that professors are not monks. They have material needs and wants like anyone else. Their status as employees, as well as professionals, places them, like any industrial or business employee, under the economic control of those who employ them.

Now there is nothing fatally incompatible with claims of professional entitlements and claims to a measure of economic satisfaction and security. Indeed, it is not at all the General Motors argument to assert that a measure of economic reward and security of employment are essential to attract qualified people into the profession and to allow those in it the freedom from economic fear needed to carry on their teaching and scholarly activities with maximum effectiveness. This much has long been part of our tradition, as witness the early assertions of the tenure claim and the activities of Committee Z.

But professors are the essence of the university enterprise, as well as its employees. They don't simply execute assigned, segmented tasks. They conceive, they plan, they govern, and they perform the processes of research and education. Indeed, it is their own work that they do, not another's. Tension is created, therefore, between these two roles. A radical imbalance in the direction of the employee role tends to create problems for the theory of the profession in a variety of ways.

Take the economic strike, for example, which some unions seeking professorial representation urge as the standard policy to resolve bargaining impasses, after the industrial model. I will not burden you with repeating the argument I have elsewhere made on this subject.[16] I will simply point out that the strike proceeds by deliberately harming the educational mission, although temporarily, in order to promote the personal employee interest, in contradiction to the service ideal of subordinating personal interest to the advancement of the purposes of the university. Its use, therefore, tends to impugn all our claimed entitlements which rest on our primary commitment to the purposes of the university, including claims to a crucial share in the government of the enterprise. More generally, the economic strike constitutes a significant compromise with the mode of persuasion implicit in arguing entitlements through appeal to shared premises. Wants backed by the threat of coercion supplant entitlements backed by reason and common commitment.

The process of collective bargaining itself, which has been gaining increased ground in higher education, raises problems even apart from the strike. In dividing the university into worker-professors and manager-administrators and governing boards, it imperils the premise of shared authority, encourages the polarization in interests, and exaggerates the adversary concerns over interests held in common. In placing the professor in the position of bargainer seeking to exact his demands from the university's managers and owners, the process of collective bargaining heavily burdens the professor's role as primary governor of the educational enterprise. Moreover, the process itself as it functions tends to remit issues which faculty should themselves determine to outside agencies, such as state and federal boards, arbitrators, and union bureaucracies. In addition, since unions rest on continued support of their constituency, the process becomes susceptible to essentially political rather than essentially academic decision-making.

Another example is the rising tendency among some professors to regard acquisition of tenure as a right of employment in the absence of demonstrated incompetence or wrongdoing. Insofar as the probationary period culminating in the tenure decision is justified under our traditional theory on the basis of the need for a substantial period of scrutiny and evaluation in order to further the goal of professorial excellence in the achievement of the missions of the university, an important tension is created by the advancement of the right to receive tenure as an employment right.

The Professor and His University as Super-Citizen

The concept of institutional neutrality was developed early as a means of protecting the freedom of the scholar and student against proprietary and public use of the university to advance ideas, viewpoints, and programs of the university's owners. But two challenges to this idea of neutrality, one dating back to World War II, the other to Vietnam, have emerged to alter the ground rules.

The first represents the effort of the federal government to use the resources of the university directly to serve governmental purposes. One dramatic form of this use is represented in governmentally sponsored and paid-for campus research. This has had two main consequences of relevance to our theme. The first is that it has tended to make universities parties, in some sense, to identifiable governmental policies— developing and building weapons, for example, or training of police for occupation control, and a variety of related programs. The other consequence has been to establish a kind of research quite alien to the *Weltbild* of the intellectual experimental station. Government-contracted research has served to limit the freedom of the researcher to choose his own lines of inquiry once the contract is made: to create in the office of project director a research manager who decides who will do the research, what turns it will take, what methods will be used, and what will be and won't be published; and sometimes to impose a seal of confidentiality on the product, thus interfering with the free flow of knowledge and ideas. It has also created a large body of researchers tied to a particular function and funding and therefore outside of tenure protection while at the same time most in thrall of the kinds of influences tenure is designed to protect against.[17]

The other challenge to the protective insulation of neutrality has come in part as a reaction to these governmental uses of the university. It represents an effort to enlist the resources and the moral force of the university to oppose governmental policies thought to be iniquitous: research in the university should be selected and selective, so that what furthers good causes would be encouraged and what furthers evil ones would not; faculties as collectivities should proclaim official positions on important issues of the day; universities should be reconstituted to serve as active workers in the quest for social justice; curriculum and instruction should include active work in the community in behalf of desirable social change so that learning becomes tied to reforming in a particular way.

Since our classic claims to autonomy from the outside and to academic freedom have rested in large part on the concept of a university as a neutral and nonpartisan haven for intellectuality, such super-citizen activist roles for the university and the faculty reduce the authority of our claims. Such roles not only catch us in the destructive embrace of orthodoxy from within, they also leave us without shelter when the wind blows from the other direction and the public and the proprietors seek to use the university in a similar way in behalf of the causes and interests and principles that they prefer. More generally, we lose the only persuasive argument we have for our extraordinary claim to support without control: a haven for research and teaching is one thing; a special lobby is another.

There is a third force of this kind which, paradoxically, is produced by the first two in conjunction. It occurs when government and the outside public, as well as the great majority of those within the university, agree on a substantive social policy and seek to use the university to further it. When this happens, we see the special purposes of the university subordinated to the university as agency of largely noncontroversial reform; dual standards of admission of students and of hiring of faculty to favor historically discriminated-against groups, reinvigorated extension programs to train people for better jobs, campus involvement with the urban community in various ways, and so on.

To a large degree, this serving the direct needs of particular interests for the public good, as opposed to simply the indirect serving of the general social interest in research, intellectuality, and general education, has always been part of American higher education—the historic land-grant college program is an example. Even so, as junior and community colleges, which have these direct service purposes as their explicit mission, are brought under the umbrella of higher education, and as universities proper increasingly feel called upon to assume community and junior college functions, it is correspondingly more difficult to insist on the university as the disengaged intellectual experiment station for the pursuit of intellectual discovery. How strong is our claim to autonomy and freedom from control by the public when we are training people for relatively routinized vocations regarded as needed in the public interest and otherwise acting in the direct service of the community as its ally in the governmental process?

In any event, there have been new and significant enlargements of the use of the university as a vehicle of social reform. Preferential hiring of minority groups and women seems to me in this category. Efforts to eradicate racial prejudice and an inherited conception of the subordinated role of women from faculty hiring are not only just and worthy. They are also wholly compatible with our theory of the profession since they are directed to eliminating nonacademic considerations from personnel decisions. But where the means used to combat prejudice along race and sex lines amount to a reverse prejudice favoring some (and hence inevitably disfavoring others) precisely along these lines, nonacademic considerations are invited back, notwithstanding the beneficence of the purpose, and our traditional theory is threatened.

These programs are troublesome enough when self-imposed. They are doubly so when imposed by government coercion. HEW [the Department of Health, Education, and Welfare], for example, routinely requires as a condition of receiving federal funds that federal contractor universities which do not employ specified percentages of women and minorities must take affirmative action to achieve the designated percentages. Specifically the university is obliged to pledge its good-faith efforts to hire women and minorities for targeted percentages of future faculty openings. Now there is argument as to whether this constitutes quota hiring—perhaps what is involved is a good-faith effort at quota hiring. But whatever we call it, I find it hard to square with the fundamental precepts of our theory, for it represents, in any event, an attempt by government to use its power to influence faculties in their hiring decisions, and on the basis of considerations, however worthy, that have no connection with professional academic criteria. There has recently been alarm in academic circles over a congressional threat to cut off federal funds for those campuses which have discontinued ROTC programs.[18] We must consider whether there is a principled distinction between this attempt at government coercion of curriculum and HEW's attempt at government coercion of academic hiring.

The University as a Body Politic

As I tried to develop earlier, our traditional theory justifies faculty autonomy within the university in terms of its special purpose and the special qualifications of the faculty in expertness and commitment to free intellectual inquiry to carry out that special purpose. As our 1966 *Statement on Government* observes, the faculty should have "primary responsibility for such fundamental areas as curriculum, subject matter and methods of instruction, research, faculty status, and those other aspects of student life which relate to the educational process" because "its judgment is central to general educational policy" and because scholars "have the chief competence for judging the work of their colleagues."[19] Challenges to this rationale, and hence to the claim of entitlement it supports, have come from a union of two related objections to the idea of the autonomous professional, one grounded on the premises of the new consumerism, the other on the premises of political democracy.

By consumerism I have in mind the rising up of the consumer of industrial products to demand his due that we associate today with the name of Ralph Nader. I take the increasing self-assertion by students to be partly a spillover from the sentiments associated with this consumer revolt: since the student too is buying a product (or someone else is buying it for him), he has a right to a say in what he gets for his money. The political democracy challenge is simply that the precepts of political democracy—that those who are governed in a political community have a right to share in its government—should be made applicable to the university community as well.

One example of the changes in thinking these new challenges occasion—in this instance the latter challenge—is the criticism of tenure, particularly from students and nontenured professors, which argues that since it vests the decision in who should receive tenure solely in the subjective judgment of those who already have it, it constitutes an unacceptable perpetuation of the power of a self-styled elite and privileged group, which is no more to be trusted because it is made up of professors.

Another example, a product of both these forces, is the rising movement for a student stake in academic decision-making. One form it has taken is the university-wide council composed of faculty, students, and administrators and vested with broad powers of government. A more pervasive form is the placement of students on faculty committees—admission committees, curriculum committees, faculty recruitment committees, tenure committees—often with the same legal status as faculty members. A related development, the new consumerism par ex-

cellence, is the official university use of student evaluation questionnaires, which, tabulated and computerized, place a stamp on the teacher
as good, bad, or indifferent for use in retention and promotion decisions.

Let me quote the response of a 1969 Oxford University committee to
one of these claims—the demand for a student share in government in
academic matters:

> We agree that there are aspects of university life where students should
> participate in strength on decision-making bodies, [e.g.] in relation to dis-
> cipline. None the less a university has as its distinctive purposes the ad-
> vancement of knowledge and teaching, conceived not as the mere trans-
> mission of knowledge, but as the development of powers of criticism and
> judgment and the adjustment of the vitalizing inter-play between research
> and teaching. In our view, no theory of legal and political rights for the
> conduct of a society as a whole, not even democratic theory, is transferable
> to the government of these distinctively academic activities. Since there
> are these distinctive purposes to be pursued, it is, we believe, plain that
> teachers equipped by skill, knowledge and experience, training and contin-
> uing professional association with a university should have final authority
> as to the manner in which they are pursued. We think that the contrary
> view can only be held by those who ignore the complexity of the truth and
> the extent to which its attainment is dependent on experience, accumulated
> knowledge, and organization.[20]

This may sound old hat and stuffy, but it reflects the view of university government which we have drawn upon traditionally to justify faculty autonomy in academic matters. When that is rejected, either our
theory or our claims need rethinking.

Concluding Observations

Some of you today may take me as simply railing indiscriminately
against the various trends and forces I have tried to describe—strikes
and collective bargaining, government-contracted research, use of the
university to advance faculty positions on controversial issues, governmental or self-imposed hiring along race and sex lines, student participation in university government. I would regret this, for my purpose
today has not been to judge these developments as such (they are not all
of a piece, and each may be defended by justifying arguments I haven't
even tried to assess[21]), but rather to point out the predicament they create for the very important theory of the profession which this Association has done so much to establish in American higher education, to es-

tablish the logical impact of advancing or permitting these developments upon the traditional theory of the profession in which our claims to entitlements are rooted.

Where these perceptions leave the profession—even assuming I am at least partly right in the incompatibilities I have identified—is not self-evident. One might choose the radical alternative of abandoning the special way in which the profession in general and this Association in particular have sought to influence the dominant forces shaping higher education; i.e., justifying professional entitlements in terms of a theory of the profession. One could argue—I would not, but some would—that we have reached the end of the road and the time has come to slough off the style and constraints of a bygone day and adopt the militant pose of demanding our wants by superior force. Some versions of unionism, not all, appear to me to be making that bid. This strikes me as a logical response, but also as an unfortunate one, for the role of the faculty in higher education is too central to its purposes, and those purposes too important for our society, to be determined by adversary combat between polarized segments of the university. We might possibly gain as employees, but the interests of higher education would not.

Another response would be to brazen it out and fudge the incompatibilities in an effort to have it both ways when we can. This, in my view, would be even less acceptable, since it would add the vice of hypocrisy to the rejection of intellectual and moral sensitivity, thus making us multiple offenders against the basic academic code. Nor would it likely work. The theory's authority would soon cease to exist and we would be left in fact with the first option after all.

A third response at the other pole would be to hang on to the traditional theory to its last logical corollary and reject every proposal and resist every circumstance which impairs its symmetry come what may and whatever the arguments. I would not wish to recommend this course any more than the first two. My reasons are partly prudential: some changes in circumstances are as little controllable as the rain—either you modify your habit or you get wet. They are also principled—we dare not treat our precepts as self-sufficient criteria of all worth, dogmas, in short, lest we become either an unmitigated self-interest group or a religious sect.

What is left for us, then? Only to face the tough and complex questions with painful awareness of their toughness and their complexity. This means, to me, resisting the temptation to embrace the popular and immediately appealing and measuring the kinds of challenges I have tried to describe in terms of their implications for the theory of the profession, which is central to our professional lives and to our reasons for being what we are. This may require some reworking of our theory at some points, but no more than is required to give their due to challenges which are worthy or inevitable and always with awareness of the need to preserve the core coherence of our professional rationale.

It would exceed the constraints of this occasion to develop my own judgments on how all the issues I have put would be resolved under this approach. It would also exceed my wisdom. But let me assert a few selective propositions as the last prerogative of an imminent has-been of the Association. Some challenges, such as the economic strike (barring the most extraordinary circumstances), governmentally coerced or even self-imposed quota-type hiring along race or sex lines, and exploitation of the professor's role in the classroom to further his own vision of social reform could, I think, find no accommodation whatsoever. Collective bargaining might be absorbed, though with some strain, into an acceptable theory of the profession to the extent it takes forms which exclude external, nonacademic control and shores up, rather than displaces, traditional faculty self-government. Vigorous and imaginative efforts to eradicate discrimination against excluded groups can and must be pressed by all means short of reverse prejudice and subordination of standards. The precept of institutional neutrality might be redefined, as Walter Metzger has suggested, to distinguish between "essentially political questions and essentially educational" (or academic or professional) "questions having political implications."[22] Student participation in university government might be expanded, provided that the faculty retains its ultimate autonomy in matters at the core of its academic mission.

If you find these few very general suggestions inadequate or ill conceived for one reason or another, I hope you will not take that as a reason to reject everything I have tried to say today. My principal objective has been to pose the predicament, not to resolve it. And if you reject these illustrative approaches to some of the answers, but accept my point that whatever decisions we make must be made with sensitive regard for preserving a viable and coherent theory of the profession, I rest my case, as I rest the Presidency of this Association, with a lighter heart.

Notes

This is the Presidential address given at the Fifty-eighth Annual Meeting of the American Association of University Professors in New Orleans, Louisiana, on May 6, 1972.

1. Cf. Howard Mumford Jones, "The American Concept of Academic Freedom," *The American Scholar,* XXIX (Winter, 1959–1960), reprinted in Louis

Joughin (Ed.), *Academic Freedom and Tenure* (Madison: The University of Wisconsin Press, 1969), pp. 224, 236–239. (Hereafter referred to as Joughin.)

2. "Academic Freedom and Tenure, 1940 Statement of Principles," *AAUP Policy Documents and Reports* (1971 ed.; Washington, D.C.: American Association of University Professors), p. 1. (Hereafter referred to as *AAUP Redbook.*)

3. 1915 Declaration of Principles. Joughin, pp. 155, 162.

4. *Ibid.*

5. 1940 Statement, supra note 2.

6. Walter Metzger, "Academic Freedom in Delocalized Academic Institutions," in *Dimensions of Academic Freedom,* ed. by Walter Metzger, Sanford Kadish, Arthur DeBardeleben, and Edward Bloustein (Urbana: The University of Illinois Press, 1969), pp. 1, 4.

7. "Academic Freedom and Tenure in the Quest for National Security," *AAUP Redbook,* p. 22.

8. "Report of the Self-Survey Committee of the AAUP," *AAUP Bulletin,* LI (May, 1965), pp. 103–190.

9. "1967 Statement on Government of Colleges and Universities," *AAUP Redbook,* pp. 33–37. See also American Association for Higher Education, *Faculty Participation in Academic Governance* (Washington, D.C.: American Association for Higher Education, National Education Association, 1967), pp. 20–22.

10. 1915 Declaration of Principles, Joughin, p. 168.

11. *Ibid.*

12. "1969 Statement on Professional Ethics," *AAUP Redbook,* p. 50.

13. "1966 Statement on Faculty Participation in Strikes," *AAUP Redbook,* p. 44. See generally "Freedom and Responsibility: A Statement of the Association's Council," *AAUP Bulletin,* LVI (Winter, 1970), pp. 375–376.

14. 1915 Declaration of Principles, Joughin, pp. 155–169.

15. I borrow the term from professor Harry Kalven, see Kalven, "The Right Kind of Anarchy," *University of Chicago Law School Record,* XVII (1969), p. 8.

16. See Kadish, "The Strike and the Professoriat," *AAUP Bulletin,* LIV (Summer, 1968), p. 160. See also "1968 Statement on Faculty Participation in Strikes," *AAUP Redbook,* pp. 42–46.

17. See "Report of the Special Committee on Academic Personnel Ineligible for Tenure," *AAUP Redbook,* pp. 28–30; Metzger, "Academic Freedom in Delocalized Institutions," *Dimensions of Academic Freedom,* pp. 1, 20, et seq.

18. See, e.g., the resolution of the American Association of Universities criticizing "the threat of coercive action to dictate to educational institutions . . . the type of instruction they should offer," *San Francisco Chronicle,* April 29, 1972, p. 6, col. 7.

19. *AAUP Redbook,* p. 36.

20. University of Oxford, Report of the Committee on Relations with Junior Members (1969), p. 23.

21. Though I have on other occasions. See, e.g., Kadish, "The Strike and the Professoriat," in *Dimensions of Academic Freedom,* p. 34; *AAUP Bulletin,* LIV

(Summer, 1968), p. 160; Sanford Kadish, Robert Webb, and William Van Alstyne, "The Manifest Unwisdom of the AAUP as a Collective Bargaining Agency," *AAUP Bulletin,* LVIII (Spring, 1972), pp. 57–61.

22. *Dimensions of Academic Freedom,* pp. 28–31.

References

American Association of University Administrators (AAUA). *Mission Statement and Professional Standards*. Tuscaloosa, AL: AAUA, 1994.

American Association of University Professors (AAUP). *Policy Documents & Reports*, Washington, DC: AAUP, 1995.

American Historical Association (AHA). *Statement on Standards of Professional Conduct*. Washington, DC: AHA, 1995.

American Political Science Association (APSA). *A Guide to Professional Ethics in Political Science*. Second edition. Washington, DC: APSA, 1991.

American Sociological Association (ASA). *Code of Ethics*. Washington, DC: ASA, 1997.

Andersen, Charles J., compiler. *Fact Book on Higher Education: 1997 Edition*. Phoenix, AZ: American Council on Education and Oryx Press, 1998.

Association of American Law Schools (AALS). *Statement of Good Practices by Law Professors in the Discharge of their Ethical and Professional Responsibilities*. Washington, DC: AALS, 1996.

Baier, Annette. "Comments." In *Philosophy and Future of Graduate Education*, edited by William K. Frankena. Ann Arbor, MI: University of Michigan Press, 1980, 82–83.

Barber, Bernard. "Some Problems in the Sociology of the Professions." *Dædalus* 92 (Fall 1963): 669–688.

Baumrin, Bernard and Benjamin Freedman, eds. *Moral Responsibility and the Professions*. New York: Haven Publications, 1982.

Bayles, Michael D. *Professional Ethics*. Second edition. Belmont, CA: Wadsworth, 1989.

Beauchamp, Tom L. and Norman E. Bowie, eds. *Ethical Theory and Business*. Fourth edition. Englewood Cliffs, NJ: Prentice Hall, 1993.

Bok, Derek. "Universities: Their Temptations and Tensions." *Journal of College and University Law* 18 (1991): 1–19. Reprinted in Bowie, 1994, 116–121.

Bowie, Norman. *Business Ethics*. Englewood Cliffs, NJ: Prentice Hall, 1982.

———. *University-Business Partnership: An Assessment*. Issues in Academic Ethics series. Lanham, MD: Rowman & Littlefield, 1994.

Boyer, Ernest L. *Scholarship Reconsidered: Priorities of the Professoriate.* Princeton, NJ: Carnegie Foundation for the Advancement of Teaching, 1990.

Bradley, F. H. "My Station and Its Duties." In *Ethical Studies.* Second edition. Oxford: Clarendon Press, 1927.

Bulger, Ruth Ellen and Stanley Joel Reiser, eds. *Integrity in Health Care Institutions: Humane Environments for Teaching, Inquiry, and Healing.* Iowa City, IA: University of Iowa Press, 1990.

Cahn, Steven M., ed. *Morality, Responsibility, and the University: Studies in Academic Ethics.* Philadelphia: Temple University Press, 1990.

Cahn, Steven M. *Saints and Scamps: Ethics in Academia.* Revised edition. Lanham, MD: Rowman & Littlefield, 1994.

Callahan, Daniel. "Should There Be an Academic Code of Ethics?" *The Journal of Higher Education* 53 (1982): 335–344.

Callahan, Joan C. "Academic Paternalism." *International Journal of Applied Philosophy* 3 (1986): 21–31. Reprinted in Markie, 1994, 113–128.

Davis, Michael. "The New World of Research Ethics: A Preliminary Map." *International Journal of Applied Philosophy* 5 (1990): 1–10.

De George, Richard T. *Academic Freedom and Tenure: Ethical Issues.* Issues in Academic Ethics series. Lanham, MD: Rowman & Littlefield, 1997.

Edgerton, Russell, Patricia Hutchings, and Kathleen Quinlan. *The Teaching Portfolio: Capturing the Scholarship in Teaching.* Washington, DC: American Association for Higher Education, 1991.

Elliott, Edward C. and M. M. Chambers, comps. and eds. *Charters and Basic Laws of Selected American Universities and Colleges.* New York: The Carnegie Foundation for the Advancement of Teaching, 1934.

Evan, William M. and Edward R. Freeman. "A Stakeholder Theory of the Modern Corporation: Kantian Capitalism." In Beauchamp and Bowie, 1993, 75–84.

Finkelstein, Katherine Eban. "The Sick Business." *The New Republic* 217 (December 29, 1997): 23–27.

French, Peter A. *Collective and Corporate Responsibility.* New York: Columbia University Press, 1984.

Friedman, Milton. "The Social Responsibility of Business Is to Increase Its Profits." *New York Times Magazine,* September 13, 1970. Reprinted in Hoffman and Moore, 1990, 153–157.

Goldman, Alan H. *The Moral Foundations for Professional Ethics.* Totowa, NJ: Rowman & Littlefield, 1980.

Goode, William J. "Encroachment, Charlatanism, and the Emerging Profession: Psychology, Sociology, and Medicine." *American Sociological Review* 25 (December 1960): 902–914.

Greenwood, Ernest. "Attributes of a Profession." *Social Work* 2 (July 1957): 45–55. Reprinted in Baumrin and Freedman, 1982, 20–32.

Hoekema, David A. *Campus Rules and Moral Community: In Place of In Loco Parentis.* Issues in Academic Ethics series. Lanham, MD: Rowman & Littlefield, 1994.

Hoffman, W. Michael and Jennifer Mills Moore, eds. *Business Ethics: Readings and Cases in Corporate Morality.* Second edition. New York: McGraw-Hill, 1990.

Hopkins, Bruce R. *The Law of Tax-Exempt Organizations.* Sixth edition. New York: John Wiley & Sons, 1992.

Hughes, Everett C. "Professions." *Dædalus* 92 (Fall 1963): 655–668.

Hutchings, Pat. *Making Teaching Community Property: A Menu for Peer Collaboration and Peer Review.* Washington, DC: American Association for Higher Education, 1996.

————. "The Pedagogical Colloquium: Taking Teaching Seriously in the Faculty Hiring Process." *To Improve the Academy* (the journal of the Professional and Organizational Development network) 16 (1997): 271–293.

————, ed. *From Idea to Prototype: The Peer Review of Teaching (A Project Workbook).* Washington, DC: American Association for Higher Education, 1995.

Kadish, Sanford H. "The Theory of the Profession and Its Predicament." *AAUP Bulletin* 58 (June 1972): 121–125.

Kant, Immanuel. *Critique of Practical Reason.* Translated by Lewis White Beck. New York: The Liberal Arts Press, 1956.

————. *The Metaphysics of Morals.* Translated by Mary Gregor. Cambridge, UK: Cambridge University Press, 1991.

Kaplin, William A. and Barbara A. Lee. *The Law of Higher Education: A Comprehensive Guide to Legal Implications of Administrative Decision Making.* Third edition. San Francisco: Jossey-Bass, 1995.

Katz, Joseph and Mildred Henry. *Turning Professors into Teachers: A New Approach to Faculty Development and Student Learning.* New York: American Council on Education and Macmillan, 1988.

Kennedy, Donald. *Academic Duty.* Cambridge, MA: Harvard University Press, 1997.

"Limitation of Autonomy is Focus of IBI Conference." *Hospital Ethics* 9 (July/August 1993): 6–8.

Ladd, Everett C., Jr. and Seymour M. Lipset. *Professors, Unions, and American Higher Education.* Berkeley, CA: The Carnegie Commission on Higher Education, 1973.

Lewis, Lionel S. and Michael N. Ryan. "The American Professoriate and the Movement Toward Unionization." *Higher Education* 6 (1977): 139–164.

Markie, Peter J. *Professor's Duties: Ethical Issues in College Teaching.* Issues in Academic Ethics series. Lanham, MD: Rowan & Littlefield, 1994.

May, William F. "Code, Covenant, Contract, or Philanthropy." *Hastings Center Report* 5 (December 1975): 29–38.

McKeachie, W. J. and Matthew Kaplan. "Persistent Problems in Evaluating College Teaching." *AAHE Bulletin* 48 (February 1996): 5–8.

Middle States Association of Colleges and Universities (MSA), Commission on Higher Education. *Characteristics of Excellence in Higher Education: Standards for Accreditation.* Philadelphia: MSA, 1994.

Modern Language Association (MLA). "Statement of Professional Ethics." In *Profession 92.* New York: MLA, 1992.

New England Association of Schools and Colleges (NEAS&C), Commission on Institutions of Higher Education. *Standards for Accreditation*. Bedford, MA: NEAS&C, Commission on Institutions of Higher Education, 1992.

Reichheld, Frederick F. with Thomas Teal. *The Loyalty Effect: The Hidden Force Behind Growth, Profits, and Lasting Value*. Boston: Harvard Business School Press, 1996.

Schurr, George M. "Toward a Code of Ethics for Academics." *The Journal of Higher Education* 53 (1982): 318–334.

Scientific Responsibility and the Conduct of Research, Panel on (Committee on Science, Engineering, and Public Policy). *Responsible Science: Ensuring the Integrity of the Research Process*, Volume I. Washington, DC: National Academy Press, 1992.

Scott, Janny. "Scholars Fear 'Star' System May Undercut Their Mission." *The New York Times*, December 20, 1997, A1, A18.

Shaw, William H. and Vincent Barry, eds. *Moral Issues in Business*. Fifth edition. Belmont, CA: Wadsworth, 1992.

Shrader-Frechette, Kristin. *Ethics of Scientific Research*. Issues in Academic Ethics series. Lanham, MD: Rowman & Littlefield, 1994.

Simon, Robert L. *Neutrality and the Academic Ethic*. Issues in Academic Ethics series. Lanham, MD: Rowman & Littlefield, 1994.

Staples, Brent. "Why Colleges Shower Their Students With A's," *The New York Times*, March, 8, 1998, section 4, 16.

Statistical Abstract of the United States 1997: The National Data Book. Washington, DC: U.S. Bureau of the Census, 1997.

Steneck, Nicholas H. "Commentary: The University and Research Ethics." *Science, Technology, and Human Values* 9 (1984): 6–15.

Wade, Nicholas. *The Science Business: Report of the Twentieth Century Fund Task Force on the Commercialization of Scientific Research*. New York: Priority Press, 1984. Reprinted as "The Erosion of the Academic Ethos: The Case of Biology" in Bowie, 1994, 143–158.

Weingartner, Rudolph H. "Ethics in Academic Personnel Processes: The Tenure Decision." In Cahn, 1990, 76–92.

———. *Undergraduate Education: Goals and Means*. Phoenix, AZ: American Council on Education and Oryx Press, 1993.

———. *Fitting Form to Function: A Primer on the Organization of Academic Institutions*. Phoenix, AZ: American Council on Education and Oryx Press, 1996.

Werhane, Patricia H. *Persons, Rights, and Corporations*. Englewood Cliffs, NJ: Prentice Hall, 1985. Reprinted, in part, in Beauchamp and Bowie, 1993, 262–270.

Index

academic administrators: calling of, 37–38, 81; described, 32–34, 46n; ethos of institutions and, 98–100; evaluation by, 56–57, 73, 88–90; faculty salaries and, 103–8; impact on institutional goals of, 39–40, 44–45; managerial responsibilities of, 33–34; obligations of, 31, 33–35, 37–38, 44–46, 67; prioritizing by, 81; as protoprofessionals, 36–37; research and, 65–68, 72–73, 75–77,79, 90–98; supervision by, 80–81, 83, 85–90; teaching and, 49–50, 52–53, 54–56, 57–58, 68; tenure decisions and, 108–16; threats to professionalism of, 119–25

American Association of Higher Education, 53n; Teaching Initiative of, 53n, 56–57, 151–62

American Association of University Administrators, 37

American Association of University Professors, 51, 52, 58, 84n, 131–34; Theory of the Profession of, 167–69, 177–78

American Historical Association, 166

Appleby, Joyce, 163, 164, 166

Association of American Law Schools, 143–49

Association of American Medical Colleges, 76n

Bok, Derek, 97

Boyer, Ernest, 77, 77–78n

Bradley, F. H., 38

Butler, Judith, 164

Butler, Nicholas Murray, 100n

Callahan, Joan C., 21

Carnegie Mellon University, 165

Cole, Jonathan, 165

collectivity: aggregate, 26–27; conglomerate, 26–29

Columbia University, 100n, 164, 165

Dartmouth College, 3–4, 5

Derida, Jacques, 165

East Carolina University, 165

Eliot, Charles, 100n

faculty: eccentricity in, 113n; evaluation of, 56–57, 73, 88–90; hiring of, 53, 57–58, 67, 159–62; need for administration of, 31–32; need for freedom of, 87, 172; nonregular, 71–72, 72n, 107–8; peer review by, 73, 85, 87, 89–90; post-tenure reviews of, 89–90; private lives of, 86–87; rewarding of, 67, 73; salaries of, 103–8; self-policing by, 52; "stars", 105–6, 163–66; supervision of, 87–88; tenure of, 108–16, 172; unioniza-

185

About the Author

Rudolph H. Weingartner, now professor emeritus of philosophy, University of Pittsburgh, has combined a career of teaching and writing with academic administration. He served as dean of the College of Arts and Sciences at Northwestern University in Evanston, Illinois, and as provost of the University of Pittsburgh. He also chaired the philosophy departments of San Francisco State University (then San Francisco State College), Vassar College, and the University of Pittsburgh. He has written many articles on topics in philosophy and higher education, as well as comments addressed to a broader audience on a wide variety of themes. His two books in philosophy are on Georg Simmel and Plato. His books on higher education topics are *Undergraduate Education: Goals and Means* and *Fitting Form to Function: A Primer on the Organization of Academic Institutions*. The former won the Frederic W. Ness Book Award in 1993. Weingartner's undergraduate degree is from Columbia College and his doctorate in philosophy from Columbia University.